surprised by
*re*marriage

surprised by *re*marriage

a guide to the happily-*even*-after

GINGER KOLBABA

Revell
Grand Rapids, Michigan

© 2006 by Ginger Kolbaba

Published by Revell Books
a division of Baker Publishing Group
P.O. Box 6287, Grand Rapids, MI 49516-6287
www.revellbooks.com

Printed in the United States of America

Library of Congress Cataloging-in-Publication Data
Kolbaba, Ginger.
    Surprised by remarriage : a guide to the happily even after / Ginger Kolbaba.
        p.   cm.
    Includes bibliographical references.
    ISBN 0-8007-5914-1 (pbk.)
    1. Remarriage. 2. Remarriage—Religious aspects—Christianity. 3. Remarried people—Psychology. 4. Divorced people—Psychology. I. Title.
HQ1018.K65 2006
646.7'8—dc22   2005032027

All epigraphs at the beginning of each chapter are taken from Quotablequotes.net and angelfire.com.

Unless otherwise indicated, Scripture is taken from the HOLY BIBLE, NEW INTERNATIONAL VERSION®. NIV®. Copyright © 1973, 1978, 1984 by International Bible Society. Used by permission of Zondervan. All rights reserved.

Scripture marked NLT is taken from the *Holy Bible*, New Living Translation, copyright © 1996. Used by permission of Tyndale House Publishers, Inc., Wheaton, Illinois 60189. All rights reserved.

Scripture marked The Message is taken from *The Message* by Eugene H. Peterson, copyright © 1993, 1994, 1995, 2000, 2001, 2002. Used by permission of NavPress Publishing Group. All rights reserved.

Scripture marked KJV is taken from the King James Version of the the Bible.

For my husband, Scott.
You often ask me if I'm still glad I married you, and would I do
it all over again.
To both questions, I offer a resounding yes.

This is my prayer: that your love may abound more and more in knowledge and depth of insight, so that you may be able to discern what is best and may be pure and blameless until the day of Christ.

Philippians 1:9–10

contents

even after land
{going forward}

"Are you sure you want to write on that topic?" my husband, Scott, asked when I mentioned to him my plans for a book about remarriage.

"Well, I know it will be difficult," I told him. "I'll need your help. But, yes, I'm sure." In my role as managing editor of *Marriage Partnership* magazine, I'd received hundreds of letters from spouses at wit's end over their remarriage. They longed to be understood, or helped and given hope, or for some—sadly—even a biblical "way out."

I wanted them to know they weren't alone. I wanted to share what I'd learned from others and in my own marriage to a man married once before.

Cue the book discussion with Scott.

"Can you handle some of the things I have to say about the topic," he asked, "and about you?"

Right. I thought. *Like I have the issues.*

"Don't worry about me, buddy," I told him confidently.

And so began the work on this book, which has been, I admit, one of the most difficult challenges I've ever tackled. Difficult because I've had to listen to my husband's nonstop jabbering about everything I should include—all the times he's been right and I've been wrong.

"One cannot write a whole book from those two times," I wanted to say. Instead I wisely urged, "If you want to be the hero, write your own book."

"That's it!" Scott has adamantly stated in any recent arguments. "I'm writing my own book, and you don't get to add anything to it."

The thing about remarriage issues or discussions or books is everyone, it seems, wants to "add to it."

First marriages, for all their trouble, have the advantage over remarriage: there isn't the history and ache of a failed relationship and a subsequent divorce. First marriages still have at least a semblance of innocence.

That innocence has been shattered when a person reaches a second marriage. Remarriage introduces issues and challenges that are unique. Couples in first marriages never have to deal with history, a different family relationship, children, and mail that arrives addressed to a spouse's ex.

Many times remarried folks feel alone, misunderstood, and stigmatized. And you wouldn't know from small-group discussions or even everyday talk in the church that there are so many remarrieds feeling this way.

A recent study by the Barna Group suggests that 35 percent of married "born again Christians" have experienced a divorce,[1] and a recent *Marriage Partnership* survey discovered 14 percent of their readers are remarried.[2]

If these statistics about divorce and remarriage are to be trusted, there are an awful lot of couples sitting in pews every Sunday who go year after year with little or no support. While there are books that focus on blended families and how to survive stepparent dilemmas, few books focus solely on strengthening a couple's remarriage. There are few remarriage church ministries too (although more are beginning to exist). And let's be honest: how many sermons have you heard that focus directly on remarriage? ("Today," says the pastor, "we're going to talk about how sex in remarriage is different and what you can do about that . . .")

It's a tough road for couples dealing with the realities of remarriage; I have stacks of letters and have met hundreds of remarried folks to prove it.

Plus I live with one.

On my wedding day, I married the man of my dreams. But he wasn't what I'd imagined while I was growing up. The man of my childhood dreams came without the baggage of a first wife and child. And although it is my first marriage, that first-marriage innocence was quickly lost because my husband was divorced. But I was in love and didn't understand fully what entering into a remarriage situation would entail.

When we were growing up, did any of us ever gaze dreamily off into space and think, *Someday, I'm going to marry a man who has an ex-wife and several children, alimony and child support payments, a whole other family and sexual history?*

We probably didn't. But here we are, married to someone who was married before we entered the picture. Or here we are, remarried ourselves—with a whole set of family pictures that don't include spouse No. 2.

Over the years, I've met and talked with numerous couples who have struggled in this area and have worked it out. I've seen enough and learned enough (both from my own marriage and from my professional work) to know what works and what doesn't. That's not to say I'm a remarriage "expert," but I'm passionate about marriage—mine and yours.

I'm not interested in failure. I don't believe you are either. Aren't you interested in making marriage work—and not just work, but succeed? Don't you want to live with joy in marriage—actually waking each morning glad that the person lying next to you is yours forever? Of realizing how much your spouse can teach you about *you*, about *us*? Not a Pollyanna-ish sort of "put on a happy face" and suffer through marriage, but a deep, lasting, honest joy for even the days when you're not happy and don't particularly like your beloved?

11

I believe this book offers a chance at that type of joy.

It isn't easy. There's no doubt about that. Remarriage can be tough. It takes stubborn will, determination, and lots of humility. It takes a realignment of our attitudes. Sometimes it even takes a suck-it-up mentality. But joy can be found and experienced. Honestly. Truly.

Speaking about what's true and honest, I'll be honest—many times while writing this book I've thought, *Who am I kidding? I can't write this.* I've had to face my own weaknesses and attitudes about remarriage. And digging up pain from the past—a hallmark of remarriage—has been grueling and heartbreaking. Situations have arisen, arguments have been had, tears have been shed.

Just a few weeks ago my husband accidentally called me by his ex-wife's name—in front of his family.

That hurt.

It also helped me reach again for those letters crossing my desk at *Marriage Partnership*, letters similar to this one: "I've searched for resources to help me in my second marriage. They aren't out there. I'm all alone . . ." Or this one: "I know there are others out there struggling, but no one has to deal with what I'm dealing with . . ."

Somehow it was a relief to know that I'm not crazy. That remarriage is tough. That I am not alone. None of us are. We would do well to lean on each other for help, comfort, and encouragement because we may never get past some things, but we can learn to deal with them better.

This book has already helped me. In my research, I've interviewed and chatted with people who vulnerably and honestly shared their thoughts, challenges, and triumphs with second and third marriages. Though the stories differ incredibly, similar threads are woven throughout.

It's become clear: *we've all made mistakes.* The apostle Paul reminds us that we've all sinned and "fall short of God's glorious standard" (Romans 3:23, NLT).

We all have regrets, things we wish we could do over, words we wish we could take back. We can't erase the past, and we can't redo it either.

But we can become better because of it. There's hope for our marriages because God hasn't forgotten about us. We still have a vital role to play in his kingdom.

"I am still not all I should be," Paul wrote when his life took on a new mission, "but I am focusing all my energies on this one thing: Forgetting the past and looking forward to what lies ahead" (Philippians 3:13, NLT).

Paul's words summarize this book.

My goal is for us to deal with and reconcile our past, let it go, and look forward to what lies ahead for our marriages. You won't find quick fixes here. The reality is that life is messy and takes deliberation or at least intention, especially in marriage. (If you've struggled through divorce, you know that.) You will find practical tips, insight, and lots of stories. Because of their candidness, I've used pseudonyms to protect the brave individuals baring their souls; to protect innocent members of my own family, I've also used a pseudonym for many of my own stories.

Some things you read in these pages may challenge, anger, or frustrate you. That's okay. I've struggled to process some of this information too! Just promise yourself you'll take the risk to try different approaches, and promise yourself that you'll enter each chapter with an open mind and heart. Ask God to help you process and hear clearly what he has to say to you about your remarriage.

By picking up this book, you've taken a great next step. I commend you for your courage. More importantly, God does too. Take his words to heart: Christ is able to do "immeasurably more than all we ask or imagine, according to his power that is at work within us" (Ephesians 3:20).

Even after.

part 1

the past

you're always taking it with you

You may have to fight a battle more than once to win it.

MARGARET THATCHER, FORMER BRITISH PRIME MINISTER

1

against all odds

{you can make it work}

I'm not a has-been. I'm a will-be.

Lauren Bacall

Okay, here's a shocker. Marriage can be rife with indifference, lack of interest, lack of concern, or just plain old apathy. There are about a hundred plus one reasons for us to leave our marriages every day.

There are times when marriage simply isn't that clichéd fairy tale. Take yesterday, for instance. My husband was upset with me because I didn't follow through on contacting a business for some work we needed done. Oh, I contacted them—by email. He'd asked me to phone them, however. To me, it's the same difference. It became such a big deal that we didn't speak to each other the rest of the evening. Supper was especially fun: there we sat at the candlelit dining room table, eating our manicotti and salad, and not talking.

These are the times when I wrestle every human instinct to pick up something and fling it. (If the manicotti hadn't been covered in tomato sauce—which I'd inevitably have to clean up—I would have flung that!)

To be fair, there's a lot of laughter and practical jokes, tickling and sex, friendship and companionship in marriage. But we already knew about that stuff when we married, right? It's the other stuff—the dark, difficult, sometimes disastrous stuff—of marriage that makes us scratch our heads in bewilderment and think, *Who is this person I married? Was there some cosmic switch after I said "I do"? I used to like this person. I used to like me with this person. Now I barely like either.*

That side of marriage was a shocker for me. Scott and I had our first whopper argument on our honeymoon. As a former actress, I admit I'm a tad bit prone to the melodramatic. So, to give me credit, when I do things, I do them big. The blow came when I discovered my beloved husband (not an actor) had the ability to "go big" too. He could yell just as loud and pout with the same commitment—as though we were both competing for an Oscar.

While we survived the honeymoon, we both discovered that our marriage wasn't going to be conflict free. (I'm still considering a class-action suit directed toward advertisers, romance novelists, Hollywood screenwriters, and anybody else who purposefully misled the public to believe that marriage was made of fairy tale dust.)

marriage isn't easy, but divorce is no picnic

Several years ago I was traveling with a freelance photographer who had just discovered his wife was sleeping with his best friend. Ugh-ly. During the entire trip my colleague was angry, devastated, and frustrated dealing with the what-ifs and the what-happeneds.

When we returned from the trip, he entered counseling right away, met with his pastor, prayed, fasted, and . . . changed. He did all the "right" things.

Still, she took up with a cowboy, became pregnant, and demanded a divorce.

He slid into depression, and his business suffered. For a while he was "homeless"—forced to move out of the home he'd shared with his wife and into his photography studio. Every time we met during this time he seemed thinner. While he still had his sense of humor, it was a little edgier; his eyes were a little less bright, his shoulders a little more slumped.

Divorce had taken its toll.

Since you're reading this book, you probably already know the devastating, anguishing, heart-wrenchingly painful process of divorce. The fact is, except in cases of "starter marriages," divorce isn't the first choice a couple makes when their marriage hits the wall. Many times it's the last resort for spouses who have dealt with the pain of a broken relationship until it just about breaks them.

The reasons for leaving a marriage don't always have to be "big": physical or emotional infidelity, abandonment, abuse, discovering your spouse has multiple mates throughout the country. Sometimes the "little" things grow into the bigger reasons: when you become upset because your husband won't balance the checkbook and you're overdrawn—again. Or you argue about how much television she watches and you're ready to smash the blasted tube. Or you feel like his mama instead of his seductress. Or your spouse is a workaholic, and you seriously consider placing her computer on eBay. Or you're stuck with being the Maid or the Babysitter while your spouse has stimulating, real (read: adult) interactions in the Outside World.

Individually, those relatively minor infractions, if left unchecked, begin to add up, until one day friends and neighbors hear of the breakup of your marriage and whisper, "We're shocked! They appeared so happy. This came out of the blue."

Yeah, right. Nothing about a divorce comes out of the blue.

Entire days, months, or worse, years go by when you feel life is unfair; when the thrill is gone, when the bedroom sees more action when you change the sheets than when you roll in them, when your spouse humiliates or ridicules you or withdraws and chooses the kids or Mom and Dad or work or golfing or shopping over you, when you feel as though your spouse doesn't support and honor and respect you. And—the worst part—when through the course of these situations God seems deafeningly silent to your pleas and pain.

Really, all you want is to wake up from this dream called life and go back to some day far in the past when life seemed less complicated, right? You just want out. Or more devastatingly, your spouse just wants out.

My husband and I have been mentoring a young man who's been married a little more than a year. His wife left him six weeks ago. She won't return calls, she stopped going to her counseling appointments, and she stopped attending church. She refuses to have anything to do with him, except to tell him, "You'll be hearing from my attorney about divorce proceedings."

"Divorce!" he told us one evening. "It feels as though someone punches me in the stomach, lets me barely catch my breath, then punches me again."

"I think one of the most difficult things about divorce is how much it changes your life," Scott told me later that night. "You never realize how much you rely on the status quo until it isn't there."

No, divorce isn't easy.

fast forward *after death too!*

After a divorce, many folks become a little rougher, a little more guarded, a little more hesitant about dreaming and falling into visions of happily-ever-after with their "soul mate."

Yet we all still long for love. We still long to be accepted and to grow old with somebody who loves us unconditionally. But for divorced folks, alongside the longing for love is the nagging thought: *is true love really possible?*

Jennifer wondered this. After thirteen years of marriage and a subsequent divorce, she didn't want to be alone and didn't want to rear her girls without a stable father figure. But as she began to date again, she saw how difficult it was to find a good fit for her. Even the Christian men she encountered had too much emotional baggage or too many red flags. She didn't want to make another mistake.

"I was tempted to believe the lie that it was too late for me to have a second chance at God's best—an awesome, God-initiated marriage," Jennifer says. "I was tempted to believe I should just take the first seemingly stable Christian guy to come along who would take me too. The prospects were frightening!"

My friend Carly told me that before she remarried she wondered, *What if it's me? What if I'm just bad at marriage? What if it's not the other person? What if I'm the one who makes wrong choices?*

When Carly met and married Rick, she entered into the new marriage tentatively. "Our marriage was different from my first one," she told me. "It felt more like we were a team. But I still had a fear that my faith in the relationship would wear off somehow; that I would grow sick of him, that it would be short lived. Or that he would begin to treat me like my first husband did."

When Scott and I were dating, he told me, "I'd rather remain single for the rest of my life than go through that hell again." We dated for six years. It took him that long to heal from his first marriage—and there are some areas where he's still healing.

Lee understands that feeling. After his twenty-year marriage ended in divorce because of his wife's multiple infidelities, he reluctantly began to date again. He met Eileen through a mutual friend, and they clicked. But as they dated, Eileen noticed his hesitance over commitment.

"Whenever we'd bring up marriage," Eileen says, "Lee would tell me how uncertain he was of remarrying. 'It isn't you,' he'd tell me on more than one occasion. 'I'd feel this way with anybody I was with.'"

21

Then one day Lee pulled from his closet a stack of cards his ex-wife had written him in the midst of her affairs. "You want to know why I'm so messed up mentally and emotionally?" he told Eileen. "Read these."

After Lee showed Eileen some of the things his ex-wife had written, she realized he was right. "His ex-wife wrote about how she loved him, how they were meant to be together forever, and how God was in their marriage—all while she was still sleeping around!" says Eileen. "She told him he was crazy for thinking she was being unfaithful, that *he* was sabotaging their marriage. I felt nauseated just reading those cards, knowing the truth behind the lies. That's when the reality hit me. It really didn't have to do with me. It had everything to do with the person I represented—a new life mate, and a new opportunity for being hurt."

Katie agrees: "I remember thinking about how bad it was to be divorced the first time, then thinking how bad it would be to be divorced *twice*."

But love is all-powerful. It draws us into the intimate community of marriage. So despite the pain and the risk, we take the leap and decide to grab hold of another chance at love, against all the odds, hoping desperately that this time will be for keeps, this time will be different. After all, our spouse is different and we are different.

It's a fresh start, a new beginning.

welcome to nonstop reality

The surprise comes when we discover the new marriage is just as difficult as the former one. That fresh start really wasn't as fresh as we'd hoped—and the cycle begins again.

Beth felt that way. Her first marriage was barely a year old when her husband, Steve, approached her and said, "I don't love you. I'm not sure I ever did. I don't want to be married anymore."

The shock and betrayal set in, and they were divorced shortly after that conversation.

So after remaining single for more than a decade, Beth finally met and married a good Christian man—and discovered he was more difficult to live with than her first husband. "He was never happy with what I brought to the marriage," she says. "We fought all the time, and I struggled with what to do next. My divorce was so painful, I couldn't imagine going through another one."

But while many people feel that same way, they still proceed to divorce again.

Some statistics show that 76 percent of second marriages, 87 percent of third marriages, and 93 percent of fourth marriages will fail within five years. While the U.S. Census Bureau and the National Center for Health Statistics are a bit more conservative on those numbers, both agree that at least 65 percent of remarriages end in divorce.[1]

If the divorce rate for remarriage is so high, we need to have our eyes wide open to be aware of what obstacles could doom our marriage, and take every precaution to avoid them. The statistics are dismal, but they are simply statistics. We can prove them wrong.

the starting point to make marriage last

In today's culture, many folks believe marriage is in major transition. Doomsayers point to the same-sex controversy, skyrocketing divorce rates, and an epidemic of infidelity as proof that the institution of marriage is in dire trouble. Even Oprah stated on one of her talk shows that "marriage is really changing."

Oprah, I disagree.

Marriages aren't changing. They're the same as they've been since Adam and Eve. Sexual, emotional, spiritual issues—none of these things are new. Americans are just more outspoken about their struggles, more ready to make public their private concerns, more willing to air their dirty laundry.

Throughout history marriage has always been a battleground, and the war has eternal consequences. When marriages fail, our community fails. Everybody is affected: children, extended family, church, neighbors, friends. Yet we can determine ahead of time not to lose the battle. We can make a commitment that we won't repeat the same mistakes in this marriage. That doesn't mean we won't carry scars or grow battle weary at times. But we will be aware of the battles, and we won't go down the same path that led to the destruction of our previous relationship. So how can we better prepare?

We can acknowledge the battle. Before my friend Sherri married Jake, they had several conversations about how difficult they knew marriage would be. Both were products of divorced homes, so they understood the nature of the battle for marriage. "We walked into marriage with our eyes open to the possibility that somewhere down the road, we were going to get hit by hardships and things that would threaten our relationship," Sherri says. The first step is to acknowledge that marriage will be a series of choices and consequences.

We can create an easy-to-remember motto. Janie and Sam's motto is simply "Not us." They came up with it just a few months into their marriage. "We felt as though we needed something like a code to remind us of our 'marriage mission,'" Janie explains, especially since Sam, along with most of his family, had experienced divorce. "Now every time we enter conflict, especially in the heat of an argument, one of us will say, 'Not us.' This lets the other person know that even though one of us is angry, even though we may not like each other right then, we're not going anywhere."

Janie and Sam's motto makes me think of the movie *Moulin Rouge*, starring Nicole Kidman and Ewan McGregor—a quirky musical that takes place in 1899 Paris. Christian (Ewan McGregor) is a young, penniless writer/songwriter who falls in love with Satine (Nicole Kidman), a courtesan who lives at the Moulin Rouge. But a duke has his sights on Satine, and trouble brews. Because of the duke's status as a financial backer of the Moulin Rouge, Satine feels forced to sleep with him. She breaks the news to Christian, who tells her that he'll write a song for them, and any time anything threatens to come between them, they will sing this song and remember their love.

Cue the orchestra.

Christian sings "their" song right there, right then: "Come what may, I will love you until my dying day." Throughout the rest of the story, that catchphrase becomes their motto as, in the end, Satine chooses fidelity to Christian and refuses to sleep with the duke.

Delia and her husband took a cue from that idea. Both in second marriages, they put together a mission statement about what they wanted from their remarriage. "When we struggle with sexual issues that stem back to my husband's first marriage," says Delia, "my emotions tend to take over and threaten to drown my resolve. It's an emotional struggle—one I have over and over." So she posted their mission statement on her desk in her home office. "One thing that has helped me," says Delia, "is that I try to remember how I felt when my husband and I first created that statement."

We can pray about our commitment. Resolve to commit your motto to God. Marriage—and especially remarriage—calls us to put all our eggs in one basket if it's going to survive. Because of the pain of a failed marriage, it becomes easy to hoard a few of the hard-boiled eggs. But love calls us to give ourselves completely to our mate, no holding back and no holding out.

Remarriage is a unique circumstance, and it proves to us that God alone is the only source of our strength. Remarriage leaves us understanding that there is no one who will never let us down—except for Christ. He is the only one we can cling to; he understands our pain, and he is always on the scene, even when we feel most alone. Ask him to join you in pursuing excellence in your marriage, and to help you stick with it when everything else encourages you to flee.

The apostle James writes, "Draw close to God, and God will draw close to you" (James 4:8, NLT). I also like the Message translation that says, "Say a quiet yes to God and he'll be there in no time."

That's really the secret to figuring out this thing called re-marriage.

but seriously: four reasons never to divorce again

1. **Marriage, for all its woes, brings comfort and security.** The truth we all know is that the dating game is over-rated—tiring and way too stressful. The great thing about being married is that you don't necessarily have to impress your spouse the way you do a date.
2. **Money is nice to have.** The government already takes too much money from us. Why pay out more to an ex-spouse? And in many divorce "settlements," your spouse will bleed you dry. (I think exes are all secretly IRS agents.)
3. **Staying married is less complicated.** Yes, you can debate this. But when kids are involved, divorce can become a nightmare. And you're probably already in one. Why add to it?
4. **A hit man is cheaper than a divorce lawyer.** This one comes directly from author Jim Watkins. He writes, "A local yokel recently paid a hit man five thousand bucks to have his wife's car blown up (with the stipulation that she was in it). A friend recently divorced his wife and will end up paying more than five hundred thousand dollars in costs during his lifetime."[2] Not that I—or Jim Watkins—advocate murder! What's even cheaper than a hit man, though? A well-qualified marriage counselor—even at one hundred dollars per one hour session. "And," Watkins points out, "you won't have to spend the rest of your life making license plates."

for *even* after

Make a covenant with God that with his help you will not entertain thoughts of, *What have I done? I deserve better than this. I'm not going to put up with this. I'm leaving.*

2

CSI divorce

{facing the death of your first marriage}

> Anybody singing the blues is in a deep pit
> yelling for help.
>
> Mahalia Jackson, American gospel singer

When I was in high school, a lady in our church died suddenly of a heart aneurysm. She was in her thirties, married, with two young children. Her death stunned the entire congregation and threw her husband into deep mourning. A year or so later, this widower met and married a woman (the whispers were that it was a rebound).

To this wise teenager, it felt as though the ghost of his first wife hung in the shadows. I remember riding home from church one Sunday morning after meeting this new woman in his life. I thought about the pain of losing someone you loved and what an awful act to follow this new woman had. *I'd rather marry someone who's divorced than someone who's widowed,* I thought. *At least if he's divorced, he chose to leave his wife. She wasn't ripped from his life forever.*

Ah, to be so young and stupid.

A decade later I learned just how foolish this idea was when I met and married a divorced man. And my girlhood thoughts have since returned to haunt me.

With the death of a relationship, it's easy (and far less painful) to look at what the ex-spouse did wrong. We can pull out the mental checklist of how we've been victimized, how our spouse didn't understand or appreciate us or meet our needs or make us happy (oh, let's count the ways). But we don't need to do any further reflection on those things—we already know them quite well!

To be sure, there are marriages in which there's an innocent party. If your spouse is a compulsive gambler and is in debt to everyone short of the mafia, then obviously you aren't responsible for that. If your spouse is physically, mentally, or sexually abusive, you didn't "ask for it." Alcoholics or drug addicts typically don't have a spouse who shoves drinks or drugs down them. If your mate has an affair, you didn't drive him to the hotel room. Those are choices for which these spouses, and these spouses alone, will be held accountable.

But no one person is entirely innocent in the death of a marriage. One person may definitely play a greater role, one may not want the marriage to end, one may fling the death blow, but two contribute.

"No divorcee can look upon all the problems of the marriage and claim, 'I was the epitome of composure and stability through all our marital ups and downs,'" Dr. Les Carter writes in *Grace and Divorce*. "The problems leading to divorce inevitably include tension, anger, miscommunication, bitterness, and insecurity. The divorcees who can say, 'I am willing to identify some definite areas for self-improvement' are the ones who have the best chance for growth."[1]

taking the hard look at . . . me

"I was a mess," says Cheri about her divorce. "My husband cheated on me, and to put it bluntly, I hated him." Cheri knew she didn't want to keep harboring these negative feelings, especially once she met Randy and started to date him seriously. So she sought professional help.

"Counseling was the hardest—and best—thing I ever did," she says now. "Not just for my relationship with Randy, but mostly just for me." By working with her counselor she recognized the role she played in her first marriage's demise.

"It centered around sex," she admits. "My husband wasn't there for me emotionally, so I wouldn't have sex with him. It caused a lot of difficulty in our marriage, and eventually he had an affair." While her husband chose to sin and to break their vows, Cheri admits that she wasn't innocent. "I used the excuse that he wasn't meeting my needs," she says. "That way I didn't feel I needed to meet his needs. It wasn't just about the affair; I really had to fess up to my part in the breakdown of our marriage."

That's not to say that every person who commits an infidelity, whether emotional or physical, does so because the spouse wasn't meeting his or her needs. We all make our own choices—and certainly no one forces us to have an affair. But, as author Sheila Wray Gregoire writes, "You could play a part in the tempting."[2]

Carol's husband had multiple affairs and verbally and physically abused her. "He was so insecure that he'd take it out on me," she says. "But I stayed in the marriage because of some bad 'Christian' counseling from my pastor. He told me, 'God hates divorce.' So I asked him, 'Does God hate dead people?' He replied that there are many martyrs." Carol wonders with incredulousness, "So I was supposed to stay married and be killed for my faith?"

It was easy for her to blame her husband for the breakup of their marriage. But when she remarried, she began to think back over that relationship. "My response to my husband was to be extremely sarcastic and disrespectful. Instead of seeking counsel, my response was to mouth off, which only helped to kill the marriage. The one area in which I have to take big responsibility was that I never realized how needy my first husband was. By the time our marriage fell apart, we weren't having sex, we weren't touching, and we were sleeping in separate rooms."

31

One night after a particularly vicious argument, they both went to their corners. He walked into her bedroom where she was sitting and said, "You don't touch me anymore."

"He looked so sad," says Carol. "I knew it wasn't about sex, it was about affection and physical touch. I just didn't touch him anymore. I knew then I didn't reach out to him and touch him, mostly because I was so angry with him and so tired of fighting. Instead, I hardened my heart toward him. Looking back, I can see that I gave up the meaningful touch long before the marriage was over."

For Phil, it wasn't about sex; it was about egos. He and his wife seemed to be vying for the title of "Marriage Martyr."

"My marriage was one continual competition in which we would one-up each other," he says. "We couldn't communicate clearly because it would turn into an argument over who had the toughest life." He remembers one argument they had over their in-laws. "We fought over whose family was the most dysfunctional! Can you believe it?" But the real problem came after each argument. They both held grudges and refused to forgive each other.

"After the divorce," Phil says, "I began to deal with what went wrong. I wanted to blame Mary for all the trouble. But when I became honest, I realized I never humbled myself to say, 'I'm sorry. I was wrong.' I didn't want to take that same pride into my second marriage."

One of the best things we can do for our new marriage? Learn from and take ownership of our past mistakes.

After all, Dr. Gary Smalley writes in his book *The DNA of Relationships*, "It's never just about the other person. The problem you have with another person is often a problem you have with yourself."[3]

Smalley tells the story of meeting a woman at an airport who told him she'd used some of his seminar videotapes to help her through a difficult marriage.[4] He asked her how their relationship was going. She replied that it didn't work out, so Smalley offered his condolences and asked what the problem was.

"The problem was him. He didn't really respect me." The woman added, "I'm in another relationship now . . . He's got problems too, but this one's better."

Smalley sums up that experience: "Sarah's story is really not that remarkable. And that's the point. Her situation is a common one, repeated in many lives over and over: 'The problem was *him*.'

"Sadly, if Sarah doesn't learn that the problem could be her—she'll soon start blaming the new man in her life for her unhappiness."

it's like dancing with the dead

Sarah's not unique. True to our human nature, we want to blame someone else, or blame "irreconcilable differences," and then move on, forget the pain we've experienced or caused. We want to bury it deep within our subconscious and leave it there to rot and decay. But when we do that, something happens. It's like those times you place something in the refrigerator and it gets shoved to the back and forgotten. (I know about this refrigerator syndrome from personal experience.)

When do we notice the forgotten item?

Usually not until the whole fridge starts to stink, right? We open the door, and out belches an odor somewhat akin to a combination of a dirty hockey outfit and roadkill.

"Whoa-HO!"

The stench tops the gag meter.

This is what happens to your past when you bury it and don't deal with it. That rotten, decaying stuff lurches into your present and makes quite the smelly scene.

Dan knows how bad the past can get when it isn't dealt with. He had an anger problem. "When my wife upset me," he says, "I'd let everything rip—verbal abuse, slamming doors, breaking items, you name it. When she filed for divorce, I blamed her completely. I didn't have the problem; she did. She made me become angry. But when my second wife also filed for divorce, and my third wife threatened it, I had to face facts. I'd never dealt with my issues, and they kept reappearing."

Those issues may not appear right away; they may take a while. But be assured they will show up.

"The real problem in second marriage occurs when people fail to identify previous problems and end up repeating them," says marriage expert Gary Oliver. "I worked with one woman who grew up in an alcoholic family, swearing she would never marry an alcoholic. Yet every one of her seven husbands has been an alcoholic."[5]

Not long ago Scott and I were walking down a country road on our way to breakfast when we came upon a dead skunk. It had decayed quite a bit. It was difficult to determine that it was a skunk except for the faint white line over its body. I walked right over to it and looked at it, fascinated. Yes, it was repulsive, but I was impressed that I didn't really smell anything.

On our return walk after breakfast, I headed back to the skunk to take another look. This time, the sun was out and beating down upon the little corpse. I learned something that day: dead, decaying skunks are still potent.

But it took a special circumstance of the sun beating down. Yes, the first time I saw the skunk, I knew there was the potential for smelly. But it took the sun showing up for me to really catch the full effect. Double nasty.

Here's the deal: we know our past issues can show up in our life and marriage, but often since it isn't a problem right then, we don't do anything about it. We leave the skunk hanging around in the background. But bring in the right circumstances, which are usually unexpected, and that skunk makes its presence well known.

What's the best way to deal with that skunk? *Run away*, you may be thinking. Nice try, but no.

Acknowledge the skunk head on, plug your nose, pick it up with a shovel, place it in a garbage receptacle, and bury it properly. Until we fully deal with our role in the death of the marriage, we've never really removed our responsibility or issues that helped kill the marriage. Sure, it's been buried—just underneath the surface. But it can and will pop up.

Only when you face the past, tackle it square on, can you understand what really went wrong in the first marriage. Not dealing with the problems in a first marriage, and maybe even further back, can be the death knoll in the current marriage, your health, all your relationships—even your relationship with your Creator.

Before Scott and I married, we spent a lot of time discussing his role in the breakdown of his marriage. He told me, "I was young, and many times I dealt with anger. Although my anger didn't justify my ex-wife's choice toward infidelity, I'm still responsible for my choices."

He's right. Nothing justifies a physical or emotional affair. It took years of hard work for Scott to sort through his issues, but that work has paid off tremendously. Those long conversations and his willingness to accept his contribution to the demise of his first marriage have made a huge difference in our marriage.

Gina also dealt with this. "When Andy and I were dating we never discussed his divorce except in terms of anger toward his wife. Now that we're married, when we get into arguments I'm ashamed to admit I think: *Is this how you treated your first wife? Is this why she left the marriage?*"

Gina took something that was dead and brought it to life.

"It used to drive me crazy," says Janie, "that my husband, Sam, would say, 'I'm sure I brought problems to my first marriage.' But he would never be specific! He'd never actually bring up anything he could work on." Because he refused to get specific, his new marriage to Janie struggled along. "I'd see problems in our marriage and wonder, *Did he deal with these in his first marriage?* But I could never find out, because he wouldn't go there."

Many of us can be tempted to think that same thing. The key is *not* to think that, which is something we can control. Otherwise, those thoughts will chip away and undermine our relationship. If we don't deal with the previous marriage, we bury it alive. And things that are buried alive somehow keep popping back up from the grave.

getting specific—and honest

One of the reasons I like the Bible is because we learn so much from the characters in the Old and New Testaments. Look at King David. I'm sure if he were around right now, he'd say, "Yes! I slept with Bathsheba, okay? Yes, I struggled as a father. But I was forgiven—do we have to continue to bring it up?!"

God told us those stories of human failings for us to learn from them. We can't get to the apostle Paul's advice in Philippians 3:13 about forgetting what is in the past until we *deal* with what is in the past.

Jennifer wanted to process what went wrong in her first marriage. During the last year of her marriage, she had an affair. "I was so angry at my husband for some of the ways he let me down that I didn't care if he found out or if I hurt him," she says. "I even hoped he'd find out, that he'd be shaken out of his marital neglect, and decide to fight for me. It totally backfired!"

Around the same time, her husband began to have an affair with Jennifer's best friend. "I experienced how it felt to be cheated on, and that was the beginning of my repentance. When he found out about my affair and I saw the depth of the pain I caused him, I was struck with the horror of what I had done. I was so deeply remorseful and repentant, I felt as if I was dying inside. That was the most barren and desolate place imaginable."

Getting specific and being honest isn't always easy. But it's worth the effort. Look at how many times Paul tells about his failures. He gives a listing of all the bad things he did—accomplice to murder, for one (Acts 22:4; 1 Corinthians 15:9). Yet, he learned from it, he was forgiven, he forgot what was past to move forward.

If you've dealt honestly with your past, you're way ahead of the game. Great job!

If you haven't dealt with your past, especially with your previous marriage, it's never too late. Taking the time to heal may be the most important thing you do for your second marriage.

"Many men and women enter second marriages by a process I call emotional collision," explains marriage expert Jim Smoke. "Struggling with the pain of a primary marriage failure, they reach out for anyone who can rescue them from their suffering and make their pain vanish." But "the 'quick fix' route leaves no time to heal the hurts of a first marriage termination, to learn what caused it to happen, or to rebuild a broken family and lay plans for the future."[6]

Promise yourself you'll commit to something beyond a Band-Aid for your past—for your sake and the sake of your remarriage; for your children, friends, church, and extended family. Most of all, do it for the sake of the plan God has for you.

Where can you begin?

Get alone. This will be time consuming, so be intentional. It's important to get away from any interruptions such as children, work, the phone, the television, computer solitaire. Schedule a chunk of time when you can be alone to think, digest, and pray.

Teresa had some friends who owned a summer cabin, so she approached them and asked if she could use their place for a weekend.

She had the right idea, according to observations from marriage experts such as David Yount. "With the advent of no-fault divorces, couples are inclined to blame 'irreconcilable differences,' without pausing to sort out those differences," Yount says. "The even higher failure rate of second and third marriages suggests that unhappy couples expend little effort in scrutinizing what went wrong the first time around."[7]

If you can afford it, go to a hotel for a day or two (internet sites such as priceline.com have some great price options you could check out). Or try a church camp or consider KOA, which has cabins you can rent. I have a friend who goes to an abbey for a weekend every year to think and pray.

Get honest. Promise yourself you won't justify or rationalize your part of the problem. The point is to take an objective look at what happened so you don't repeat the same problems in your current marriage. It's important to remember this honesty isn't about pointing the finger and calling ourselves "bad." It isn't about piling on guilt. It's simply an exercise in recognizing mistakes and sins in order to learn from them, not repeat them, and become better individuals and spouses. So it's important to avoid the "yes, but" syndrome. You know, "*Yes*, what I did was wrong, *but* my spouse made me do it. . . . He made me angry. . . . She never gave me respect." And the list goes on.

Pray. This is an essential step. You may be digging deep into pain, so it's important to ask God at the outset, and all the way through, to protect you. This is an opportune time for those nasty, pesky thoughts to intrude that can either put the guilt trip on you or really make you angry about your past.

It's okay to deal with your emotions, but you want to remain as objective and rational as possible. No justifications or rationalizations. You're on the quest for truth.

Invite God to work with you through this period. Try praying, "God, I don't want my past to control my present. I don't want to live under the chains of what happened in the past. I want to be free to live in a God-honoring marriage. Protect my thoughts, guide them, and help me stay focused on what you would have me learn."

Play Twenty Questions. Take a piece of paper or a journal, and answer the following questions. Make a point not to blame your ex-mate. Deal strictly with your part in the marriage. If you're struggling, ask God to open your mind, to highlight certain areas where you failed the marriage or where you played the part of accomplice. It's important to answer the questions as honestly, objectively, and specifically as you can.

- If my ex-spouse were to evaluate me as a mate, what would he/she say? Why?
- Whether or not I agree with the assessment, what can I learn about myself if I accept at face value his/her accusations?
- What went wrong in the marriage?

- What role did I play in the dissolution of my previous marriage?
- Were there times during my marriage when I could have asked for forgiveness and didn't?
- Were there times when I could have made things right, but my pride kept me from doing it?
- Were there times when my spouse asked me to do something and I refused?
- Were there times when I reacted inappropriately to my spouse's actions?
- Whether my ex is right or wrong, what would he/she say about me in our marriage?
- What would my ex-spouse say was one of our major problems?
- What would my ex-spouse say was the final straw to our marriage dissolution?
- What am I feeling about that marriage? Why?
- Why am I focusing that feeling toward my spouse?
- Did I have unrealistic expectations toward my ex?
- Did I treat my spouse like a soul mate or like a role mate?
- Did I give up on the marriage too quickly?
- Did I do everything in my power to save the marriage?
- Do I harbor unforgiveness toward my ex?

Journal. One good way to work through these issues is to start a journal. Write about the root problems and issues and how you played a role. Again, the goal is not to rehash; it is to learn.

"Keeping a journal was a lifesaver for my remarriage," says Linda. She "free formed," a type of writing in which you basically "vomit" onto the page, writing everything that comes to mind. No rules, no worries about correct grammar or what anybody would think if they read it.

After she wrote, she put away the journal for a week, then looked at it again, adding more of her faults as they came to mind.

"I put it away again for another week," she says, "then pulled it out, looked at it, and discovered how truly heartbroken I was. At that point I was able to become honest with God and seek forgiveness. The most amazing thing happened when I did that. I felt free—truly and completely free!"

Seek professional Christian counseling. There's nothing that works as well as having an objective person help guide you through this process. A counselor can help you become honest and hold you accountable, and can aid in your healing.

"Anybody coming out of a marriage, regardless of whose 'fault' it is, should go to counseling," says Carly, whose first husband committed adultery. "Even a few sessions just to sort out what went wrong and what you can learn can make an amazing difference in your remarriage."

Once you've discovered your part in the dissolution of your marriage, you'll be aware of those elements popping into your current marriage and will be able to handle them constructively.

If you need a good referral for a counselor in your area, check out the American Association of Christian Counselors at www.aacc.net or the American Association of Pastoral Counselors at aapc.org.

for *even* after

List some problem areas you dealt with in your previous marriage, then list a corresponding Scripture verse to help you work through those areas. Next to "critical spirit," for instance, you may write, "Philippians 4:8–9: 'Whatever is pure, whatever is lovely, whatever is admirable—if anything is excellent or praiseworthy—think about such things. . . . And the peace of God will be with you.'"

3

the GOD factor

{grabbing hold of grace}

Many a humble soul will be amazed to find that the seed
it sowed in weakness, in the dust of daily life, has blos-
somed into immortal flowers under the eye of the Lord.

Harriet Beecher Stowe

Divorce and remarriage are funny things. Some Christians say
divorce is a sin. Others say it isn't, but it displeases or saddens
God. Yet others go so far as to say, "God wants us to be happy,
so he's okay with divorce."

In a recent study done by the Barna Group and reported in
Christianity Today, 52 percent of "born again Christians" disagree
with the statement, "When a couple gets divorced without one of
them having committed adultery, they are committing a sin."[1]

Whatever.

The one thing we do know for certain: divorce isn't mentioned
with much fondness in the Bible.

but I'm already divorced!

I can almost hear you thinking, *Okay, since I'm already divorced, what am I supposed to do with this, other than feel guilty?*

I don't know the circumstances of your divorce and remarriage. My husband, Scott, sought a divorce after his wife had multiple infidelities. While he was free to remarry, he still had to work through forgiveness and faith issues.

So why deal with the topic of divorce when we're already past that point? Why rehash it? Why is this chapter even in a book on remarriage? What does this have to do with anything?

Great questions.

Whatever your belief about divorce and remarriage—whether you think divorce is a sin, an inconvenience, or an unfortunate event—if we want our remarriages to succeed, if we want to experience blessings in our future, if we want to stay positively and powerfully connected with God, then we need to understand what God has to say about divorce and our role in it.

I'm convinced that divorce is a death. And death affects every part of our lives—including, potentially, our spiritual lives. Until we deal with that death and bury it properly, we don't give our new marriage a real chance at success. We don't allow God to work fully and completely in our lives.

I'm interested in making sure that your marriage today has everything it needs to succeed, to thrive, to bless others, and to be used by God in a tremendous way.

We can't talk about relationships in a Christian context without dealing with what the Bible has to say about divorce and remarriage.

the famous Malachi verse

Before we explore my premise that divorce is a death, let's do a refresher course on some familiar Scripture passages.

In the Old Testament, the prophet Malachi writes, "'I hate divorce!' says the LORD, the God of Israel" (2:16, NLT).

Most of us have heard that verse bandied about more times than we care to count. We've read it and heard sermons on it; we've had it recited to us by well-meaning friends and family. And let's face it: this is not the most touchy-feely of verses. Through that whole chapter the Lord, through his prophet Malachi, doesn't mince words.

What's even more interesting is the context of the verse: Malachi is actually writing about a call to faithfulness and loyalty. Look at what the verses surrounding that famous one say:

> You cover the LORD's altar with tears, weeping and groaning because he pays no attention to your offerings, and he doesn't accept them with pleasure. You cry out, "Why has the LORD abandoned us?" I'll tell you why! Because the LORD witnessed the vows you and your wife made to each other on your wedding day when you were young. But you have been disloyal to her, though she remained your faithful companion, the wife of your marriage vows. Didn't the LORD make you one with your wife? In body and spirit you are his. And what does he want? Godly children from your union. So guard yourself; remain loyal to the wife of your youth. "For I hate divorce!" says the LORD, the God of Israel. "It is as cruel as putting on a victim's bloodstained coat," says the LORD Almighty. "So guard yourself; always remain loyal to your wife."
>
> You have wearied the LORD with your words.
>
> "Wearied him?" you ask. "How have we wearied him?"
>
> You have wearied him by suggesting that the LORD favors evildoers since he does not punish them. You have wearied him by asking, "Where is the God of justice?"
>
> 2:13–17, NLT

Did you catch all that? Look at that passage in another translation, the Message:

> You fill the place of worship with your whining and sniveling because you don't get what you want from GOD. Do you know

43

why? Simple. Because GOD was there as a witness when you spoke your marriage vows to your young bride, and now you've broken those vows, broken the faith-bond with your vowed companion, your covenant wife. GOD, not you, made marriage. His Spirit inhabits even the smallest details of marriage. And what does he want from marriage? Children of God, that's what. So guard the spirit of marriage within you. Don't cheat on your spouse. . . .

You make GOD tired with all your talk.

"How do we tire him out?" you ask.

By saying, "GOD loves sinners and sin alike. GOD loves all." And also by saying, "Judgment? GOD's too nice to judge."

Malachi says some pretty rough things in these verses.

First, he says our tears and groans (and whining and sniveling) don't make a dent in God's position. We cry out to God and feel as though our prayers are hitting the ceiling and bouncing back.

Second, he says God doesn't accept our offerings. He isn't impressed by all our good deeds and "sacrifices." He wants us to do right.

Third, he says God has abandoned us.

Ouch.

Old Testament prophets weren't exactly pictures of sweetness and light. They pretty much just blurted it right out there. Malachi writes: "You cry out, 'Why has the LORD abandoned us?' I'll tell you why!" (The Message). He doesn't say, "There, there, God hasn't abandoned you. He's still here. He just wants you to be happy."

Then, if it isn't bad enough to say God hates divorce, Malachi backs it up with, "It is as cruel as putting on a victim's blood-stained coat."

The New King James Version says, "He hates divorce, for it covers one's garment with violence."

The New International Version says, "I hate divorce . . . and I hate a man's covering himself with violence as well as with his garment."

Theologians debate what the violence part of that means. Some suggest that it's separate from the divorce matter. That God is talking about violence such as domestic violence. Some say it is still in reference to the divorce matter—saying divorce is as bad as violence. Either way, God connects violence with divorce. One is as bad as the other. Obviously, divorce is a serious matter to God.

the famous Jesus sayings

But what about what Jesus has to say about divorce? Jesus also doles out some strong words.

When the Pharisees asked Jesus if divorce was lawful under any and every circumstance, Jesus responded: "Moses permitted you to divorce your wives because your hearts were hard. But it was not this way from the beginning. I tell you that anyone who divorces his wife, except for marital unfaithfulness, and marries another woman commits adultery" (Matthew 19:8–9).

The Message translation puts it this way: "Moses provided for divorce as a concession to your hardheartedness, but it is not part of God's original plan. I'm holding you to the original plan, and holding you liable for adultery if you divorce your faithful wife and then marry someone else."

It's important to note that Jesus said Moses didn't command divorce but allowed it.

What's sad, though, is divorce was allowed because the people had hard hearts—not exactly the thing I'd want anybody to say about me. That's the kind of thing said about Ebenezer Scrooge, and the Grinch, and Pharaoh of the Old Testament—even after the Passover when his firstborn son was killed.

No, God's original intention for marriage, his plan before the fall in the Garden of Eden, was that husbands and wives would stay together their entire lives. He designed marriage to be the showcase of how the Trinity works together—how each person in the Trinity brings a unique perspective and purpose, making the Trinity "one" in spirit.

Divorce was not part of that plan. Period. In fact, divorce never entered the picture until sin entered the picture. Death also never entered the picture until sin occurred. That's also important because in marriage God unites two people into one (Matthew 19:5). So when a divorce occurs, there's no longer that "one." There is death.

If you look throughout the entire Bible, you'll see another important thing: pictures of community. That's because God created us for relationship. He started community in the Garden of Eden by creating Adam and saying, "It is not good for him to be alone." If you notice, that's the first time God says something is not good; everything up to that point was good.

So what else did Jesus want us to notice about marriage and divorce?

He said that if we get a divorce against a faithful spouse, we commit adultery—adultery, even if we're technically remarried. That's a Ten Commandment, a biggie.

Jesus didn't mince words when he claimed that marriage is tough—and it's permanent.

My favorite part of this passage is what the disciples say afterward: "If this is the situation between a husband and wife, it is better not to marry" (Matthew 19:10, NLT).

I have to laugh at this because haven't most people thought that? *If only I'd known how tough marriage was, I'd have stayed single!* With Jesus's words, the disciples realized the seriousness of the commitment. And Jesus agrees! He says, "Not everyone is mature enough to live a married life. It requires a certain aptitude and grace. . . . But if you're capable of growing into the largeness of marriage, do it" (Matthew 19:11–12, The Message).

making sense of it

The Bible is clear that God wants a positive, fulfilling relationship with us. He wants to bless and lavish us with his love, and grow us strong in character and virtue. He's passionate about his relationship with us! Nothing will change his love for us. Nothing.

The apostle Paul reminds us of this fact. He writes:

> I am convinced that nothing can ever separate us from his love. Death can't, and life can't. The angels can't, and the demons can't. Our fears for today, our worries about tomorrow, and even the powers of hell can't keep God's love away. Whether we are high above the sky or in the deepest ocean, nothing in all creation will ever be able to separate us from the love of God that is revealed in Christ Jesus our Lord.
>
> Romans 8:38–39, NLT

However, often leading up to divorce, through the course of it, and amid its aftereffects, our hearts become hard, as Jesus pointed out. We close our minds and affections to our spouse, and, unfortunately, often to God. We're steadfast in our decisions, and that's that.

While we can divorce ourselves from our spouse, it's a little trickier to extricate ourselves from God's Spirit, who continually leads us to forgive, reconcile, and do right. It's trickier because we're suddenly not in balance. How can we be? When we ignore God's voice and his pleadings to us, we're not on the right footing with him, and then we're not in balance with anything.

Dr. Gary Smalley explains:

> When your relationship with God is out of balance, you can't see yourself properly and you lack the power to change or enjoy life as he intended. And it's more complicated when the other person also has an unhealthy relationship with God. Then neither of you is seeing yourself clearly. What happens then is that you begin to react to each other for the wrong reasons—sometimes with an inflated sense of who you are, and other times with a deflated sense of who you are. If neither of you can see yourself accurately, how do you expect the relationship to work?[2]

Diana was miserable in her marriage. "We were incompatible from the start," she says. "Everybody told me that, but I was in love and didn't want to hear anything that went against my plans. I wish I had listened. Instead I got married and spent the next ten years miserable." Diana couldn't take it anymore and decided to pursue a divorce.

"I knew I really didn't have an 'out' in my marriage. My husband was faithful. We just had major incompatibility problems," she says. "So when I'd sit in church and hear about grace and forgiveness and our need to offer them to others, I didn't want to have anything to do with that. Once again, I wanted my way."

Diana closed her ears to God's whisperings and divorced her husband.

After that, she received the surprise of her life. "I figured I would do this thing, and God would forgive me, and everything would be great." The problem was Diana's heart was still hardened toward her ex-husband and, frankly, to God.

"I sidestepped God," she admits. "My life was out of balance, and I couldn't figure out why there was a problem. I grew depressed. My children started to rebel, and I started to have financial problems. But hey, I got my way, didn't I?"

She walked away from God, and in turn, walked away from love, joy, peace, and health.

The truth is, though divorce may be acceptable in certain cases, and God allows us an out, it's still not his preferred way. Divorce is accepted because the soul of the marriage has been tainted, crushed, and wounded.

In the case of a divorce for reasons other than "acceptable proceedings," we've essentially tied God's hands to blessing us. It's not that he doesn't want to bless our lives; we've just made it so that he can't. We've put a barrier between us and God. We've stepped away from his will.

In 1 Peter 3:7, the apostle Peter talks to husbands about how they should treat their wives: "Husbands . . . be considerate as you live with your wives, and treat them with respect as the weaker partner and as heirs with you of the gracious gift of life." But there's a consequence if you don't: do this "so that nothing will hinder your prayers."

If withholding basic respect and consideration can hinder our prayers, how much more are our prayers hindered when we divorce because of hardened hearts?

Because God is a holy God (Isaiah 43:15), and because "in him was life" (John 1:4, KJV), he simply won't co-dwell, if you will, with death. As Malachi stressed, he doesn't abandon us because he desires to punish us—and he would never abandon us. But he can't get through to us because of our actions. We are the ones who have pushed him away. When we tie God's hands, it's as though we have this dark cloud continually hanging over our remarriage.

so what to do?

How can we untie God's hands? How can we ask and receive God's blessings on this new marriage?

Go back to Malachi for the first part.

Get right with God. Notice Malachi's words: "'Return to me, and I will return to you,' says the LORD Almighty" (3:7). God desires that we confess our part in the death of our marriage. That's why we discussed our role in the previous chapter.

A change of mind leads to a change of action, states the NIV Thematic Reference Bible in defining repentance. The definition includes this:

> At its heart, repentance involves a sincere turning away from sin in order to serve God. Scripture identifies the main elements of repentance as being a turning away from sin toward God, a confession of the sins committed, sorrow for sins in question. Repentance must be genuine; if this is the case, it opens the way for God's blessing, full forgiveness and restoration to fellowship with God.[3]

Pick up that journal we discussed in the previous chapter and read through it, with an eye to repentance. List to God where you messed up in your last marriage. Take responsibility for those things you did by being honest and specific. If you don't feel repentant, tell God that too! After all, it's not as though that would be a surprise to him—as though he doesn't already know what we feel. Tell him you want forgiveness, but you don't feel remorse for the death of your marriage and for your role in it. That's okay. Ask God to melt your heart. God calls us to be obedient to him. When we take the first step, God will meet us there, and he will do the rest of the work.

Sometimes we are innocent too. If your spouse was unfaithful to you, you didn't force her or him to walk out of the marriage. But if you still deal with anger or unforgiveness toward an ex-spouse, you need to get that straight with God. Anger and unforgiveness can turn into bitterness. We need to work to forgive and then let it go. If not, it will affect every part of our soul; it will affect our relationship with Christ and our relationship with our current spouse. Willow Creek Community Church's senior pastor, Bill Hybels, spoke about confession in his study of 1 John. He called it the Four A's:

- Admit that I messed up.
- Agree with God that it's a problem.
- Ask God to clean my slate.
- Accept that he has.

Get right with our ex. Forgiveness is the biggie. Forgive and forget? Nope. Forgive, yes. We all know we can never forget. So this doesn't mean you and your ex become bosom buddies and let bygones be bygones. It's what we do with our memories that makes a difference. In his excellent book *Forgiving and Reconciling*, Everett Worthington Jr. writes, "[When I forgive] I will not forget; I will remember differently."[4]

God can forget because he doesn't need to remember or learn ✒
anything from the situation. I believe God allows us to remember things because we can learn and grow from them. Because that's part of his plan for us to remember his grace and for us to grow in our character to become more like Christ. The process of forgiveness isn't cheap. It's about saying, "If I believe in God, if I believe God is who he says he is, then I have to take him at his word." If he is a God of justice (Isaiah 30:18), one who will fight for us (Exodus 14:14; Deuteronomy 3:22), then we can let him deal with our ex-spouse. We can forgive, trusting that God will do his job much better than we can.

Ask God to bless this new marriage. We know remarriage isn't the ideal situation. There's a loss of innocence and newness. But God promises that he will work "for the good of those who love him, who have been called according to his purpose" (Romans 8:28).

Renew your commitment to honor your vows to your current spouse.

God does that for us, the prophet Micah reminds (7:19): "You will again have compassion on us; you will tread our sins underfoot and hurl all our iniquities into the depths of the sea."

for *even* after

"Write a letter to God, detailing all the wrongs in that marriage you want God to forgive you for. Pray over it. Tear it up and throw it away. Then take it out of the trash and tape it together. Embellish it. Write even more bad stuff. Then tear it up again and throw it away. Keep doing that until you know that God has forgiven you."

—Carol, remarried four years

4

forgiveness

{exercising the ultimate trust}

We talk a good forgiving line as long as somebody else
needs to do it, but few of us have the heart for it while
we are dangling from one end of a bond broken
by somebody else's cruelty.

Lewis B. Smedes

My brother-in-law is a chiropractor/nutrition specialist, and one evening as my husband and I were having dinner with him we began to discuss how the past affects our present and our future. He told us about a woman who'd been referred to his office that day.

"Her health is a mess, and she's only thirty-six years old," he said. She'd been divorced and was currently involved in another difficult relationship.

"When I asked her what went wrong in her first marriage," he told us, explaining that it's common in any severe health case to recount past experiences, "she said that her husband physically abused her and cheated in their relationship."

Then he asked what her childhood was like and how her father treated her.

After a moment's hesitation, she told him that her father had sexually abused her from ages eleven to seventeen.

"Have you ever dealt with that issue?"

"Look," she told him. "I don't want to talk about my father. I've dealt with my past in counseling. I've bottled that period of my life and thrown it over a bridge. I'm not going to dredge it up to talk about it. It has nothing to do with my health."

Come to find out, her new relationship was also a nightmare. She was again experiencing an abusive and adulterous relationship.

Is there a pattern here?

"Let's make this easy and lump your health and relationship issues together," my brother-in-law counseled the woman. "The reason your health and intimate relationships are deteriorating is because you've never dealt completely with the past. Until you do, until you forgive your father, your first husband, and even yourself, you'll never heal and move into a healthy, God-honoring state."

She couldn't bring herself to open up the past and truly break free from it. She found it too painful. So to avoid the pain, she was, in fact, killing herself.

why forgive?

My brother-in-law's patient was a victim. Many of the problems in her first marriage stemmed from the fact that she hadn't dealt with her past. While she can't change the past, she can take responsibility for what she does with it.

The same is true in remarriage. We can never truly be free in our remarriage until we've broken the chains of the past. That means we have to forgive and seek forgiveness where necessary. We forgive so that God will forgive us. In Matthew 6:14–15, Jesus tells his followers: "If you forgive those who sin against you, your heavenly Father will forgive you. But if you refuse to forgive others, your Father will not forgive your sins" (NLT).

Another version puts it this way: "In prayer there is a connection between what God does and what you do. You can't get forgiveness from God, for instance, without also forgiving others. If you refuse to do your part, you cut yourself off from God's part" (The Message).

Forgiveness isn't about condoning what the other person did. It's about saying, "I choose to forgive you. I trust that God, who is just, will seek justice for me. So I can let you go, knowing that you are ultimately in God's hands."

In her book *Radical Forgiveness*, author Julie Ann Barnhill writes: "Forgiving someone who betrayed you means that you have taken the reins—you have decided to let go of the hurt, the anger, the fear, the bitterness. And that you have decided to go in a different direction instead of letting the person or situation control your life."[1]

We forgive to free ourselves from that person's control. We forgive to become mature in our faith. We forgive so that God will forgive us.

I can hear you thinking, *It's not fair! You don't know how badly he hurt me! Why should I let that person off the hook? Where's the justice in that?*

The truth is that many times life just isn't fair. We all live with the consequences of another person's sin. (Do Adam and Eve ring a bell here?) However, God's desire is for us to forgive.

God will not forget us or our pain. The author of Hebrews reminds us, "For we know him who said, 'It is mine to avenge; I will repay'" (10:30).

what forgiveness looks like

How do we actually forgive? It's a process, but the steps are identifiable—and doable.

Acknowledge the hurt. This may seem obvious, but too often many of us move into the denial mode: *That hurt didn't really matter. It's over now, anyway. I'm remarried.* Denying our pain doesn't make the hurt disappear. It simply stifles it. Facing the hurt from the former marriage will help us come to grips with it.

Pray. Here's the reality: without supernatural help, we cannot forgive someone who's hurt us. Within our own flesh, we simply can't do it. Our instinct is to exact retribution, to demand the pound of flesh. So instead, we need to pray, sometimes through gritted teeth, for help to forgive.

When Carol realized the importance of forgiving her ex-husband, she began to pray for him. "At first, my prayers were that it would be a rainy, slippery night and he'd crash his motorcycle!" That's not a prayer I'd recommend, but at least she was honest. How many of us have at least temporarily lost our sanity and thought bad things about the ex? Sometimes we simply have to ask God for the strength just to start the forgiveness process. Here are three specific things to pray for:

- To protect your mind, to focus on the forgiveness aspect, not the anger and hurt aspect. When your mind starts to wander into the negative, and it seems to dig deeper into bitterness, which is the opposite of forgiveness, pray 2 Corinthians 10:5: "We demolish arguments and every pretension that sets itself up against the knowledge of God, and we take captive every thought to make it obedient to Christ."
- For the Holy Spirit to be your comforter. Digging up this pain can go deep and can bring torment, anger, and even more hurt. Yet God is our protector and comforter. The psalmist reminds us, "'Because he loves me,' says the Lord, 'I will rescue him; I will protect him, for he acknowledges my name. He will call upon me, and I will answer him, I will be with him in trouble, I will deliver him and honor him'" (Psalm 91:14–15).
- For the ability to empathize with the person who hurt you. Ask God to allow you to see things from the offender's point of view. Try to imagine what made that person hurt you. If you still struggle with the thought of forgiving, that's okay.

God knows your heart. Ask him to soften it. Ask him to help you become willing. Then (take a deep breath here) begin to pray for your offender. Once Carol realized the motorcycle crash idea wasn't too God-honoring, she decided to change her prayers. "I was determined to forgive my ex-husband, so I started to pray for him. I started to pray that he would continue to be a good father to our children. I prayed that he would succeed in his work and family relationships. And you know what? God began to melt my heart—it took years, but he did it! And recently I've seen my ex soften toward me too."

Strive for humility. What works best is to think of the times you've received forgiveness. I can't tell you how many stupid, mean things I've done and said, and have still been forgiven. And how many times has God forgiven me? My life is just one big long list of "forgivens." If God will forgive me, then surely I can forgive someone who has hurt me. In a recent interview with Max Lucado, I asked him about forgiveness and grace in marriage. He told me that when God forgives, it's as though we're standing under the Niagara Falls of grace. If that's what God does for us, he said, "what others need from us is like a teaspoon of grace in comparison."

Start with the smallest and easiest offenses. Sally wasn't ready to forgive her husband for his "indiscretions." But she knew she needed to forgive him. So she decided to forgive him for lying to her when he said he'd attend church with her, then never did. "I was able to forgive a lie easier than forgiving the affairs." Once you've worked through the small stuff, the bigger things may be easier. Carol started by forgiving her ex for not allowing her any contact with his family. "I loved Natt's family, and they loved me. He was so angry during the divorce that he told me I would have to give back his name and never again have contact with his family. It was painful to have to give up his family. But that was the place where I started to forgive Natt."

Realize the offender has bigger problems than you to worry about. If your spouse was sexually unfaithful to you, you're the least of his problems. We have a just God to whom your ex will have to answer. I'm a firm believer in the "what goes around comes around" theory. Some people call it karma. I call it the natural consequences of sin. Sin's effects ripple out, but then, like a boomerang, they always come back—usually faster and fiercer than before. I've often found it easier to forgive when I realize that someday that person will be accountable for everything said and done, and so will I.

Anticipate that the wounds will still hurt. Somehow we get the idea that once we've forgiven, we'll magically forget the painful experience. Yet when the memory emerges again, we think we haven't truly forgiven. That's simply not true.

Know that you'll remember at least some of the pain from your past for the rest of your life. Everett Worthington Jr., an expert in the study of forgiveness, explains:

> The hurt is burned into our brain. It becomes part of our wiring. The sight of the person's face, the sound of his or her voice, images of the acts of harm, the angry and fearful emotions of our immediate reactions, and the memories of subsequent events are recorded. It isn't really like storing a program in a computer; it's more like changing the circuitry of the computer. The biochemistry of our brain changes.[2]

There is hope, as Julie Ann Barnhill writes.

> The tough truth is, forgiving isn't forgetting. When we forgive someone, we do not forget the hurtful act, as if forgetting came along with the forgiveness package, the way strings come with a violin. If you forget, you will not forgive at all. You can never forgive people for things you have forgotten about. You need to forgive precisely because you have not forgotten what someone did. . . . The really important thing is that we have the power to forgive what we still do remember.[3]

Cling to the forgiveness. Every time you recall the painful incident, remind yourself that you've forgiven. Eventually, the pain will diminish.

asking forgiveness

Sometimes it will be our responsibility to seek forgiveness from our ex-spouse.

Jennifer felt God leading her to apologize to her ex-husband for certain areas in which she failed him as a wife. "I didn't respect my first husband at times, I didn't have confidence in him, I was unfaithful to him in my thoughts throughout our marriage, and sometimes I was controlling with anger. I put too much pressure on him to succeed," she admits. "I also had a hard time forgiving him when he hurt my feelings, and I would punish him by withdrawing. God showed me how much I had beaten him down by my attitudes and how much I had hurt his self-esteem. When God revealed to me these things, I felt terrible."

Each time God would open her eyes to a particular area, Jennifer realized her remorse and would contact her ex to apologize. She would be specific about what she felt she had done wrong. "At first, he was suspicious," she says. "But then he began to see I was truly sorry. His heart softened too. Now we get along much better."

Although it will take some ego-bruising and some concerted scaling back on the pride front, when we humble ourselves, God hears and responds to our obedience, whether our ex chooses to accept our repentance or not.

If you're not comfortable talking with your ex, that's okay. Write a letter. Remember, this isn't to offer excuses, reasons, or justifications—that stuff goes into that "yes, but" syndrome we discussed earlier. You can make this letter short and sweet: "I did this; I realize now how much my action hurt you; I was wrong; please forgive me."

how important is reconciling?

God desires for us to reconcile whenever it's possible. This does not mean we should become best buddies with our ex. But we should at least consider being cordial to that person.

Many exes reconcile for the sake of the children, so they'll spend holidays together or vacations or dinners. If you feel God leading you in that direction, go for it. Obviously, you will be tentative at first. And only do this if your current spouse is okay with the idea. Keep praying through the decision and experience.

However, there will be times when reconciliation isn't the wisest option. A stalking ex-spouse who's threatened to kill you is probably not worth the risk of reconciliation. Neither are "toxic" people, those folks who still have the ability to cause you pain. For instance, as Lee worked through his forgiveness issues with his ex-wife, he prayed about reconciling and decided against it. "I don't wish her harm," he says. "I don't harbor any ill will toward her. I've forgiven her and have moved on. But she broke so much trust with me by manipulating me, having multiple affairs, then lying about them, that I don't feel any interest in pursuing a relationship with her."

Sam agrees. "Everything that comes out of my ex-wife's mouth is a lie," he says. "Throughout our marriage she lied. She had affairs, and she lied. She abandoned our children, and she lied. Now that we're divorced, she still lies about silly things. My wife and I have caught her in numerous lies. I don't see how I can put myself or my wife into a situation that deals with that all the time."

While sometimes reconciliation isn't an option, that doesn't mean we declare hostile ground. God understands relationships, but he still desires that we remain loving in our encounters.

Seriously consider whether or not reconciliation is an option for you and your spouse. Pray about it. Listen to the soft whisperings of the Holy Spirit. If you choose to reconcile, it may be treacherous leanings for a while. You'll need to get your spouse on board. If you forgo reconciliation, don't beat yourself up over it.

In either case one thing is certain: don't do this behind your mate's back or you may end up with two ex-spouses. At this point in your life, your current spouse is your priority. And whatever your choices, you can ask God to guide and care for all those around you.

Sound too good to be true?

Janie, remarried for five years, thinks not. "Forgiveness isn't a boundary-free ticket to allow my ex to continue moving outside the bounds of God's will," she says. "As Christians, we often get sucked into the mentality that we simply forgive willy-nilly and allow that person to keep hurting us. If we do that, we need to forgive ourselves for being a sucker! Christianity isn't equal to being a doormat. I can forgive and then get away from that situation or person. I can forgive my husband's ex-wife, but that doesn't mean I want to go shopping with her and meet every week for lunch. I can still forgive and keep my distance."

for *even* after

Need help empathizing? Try this exercise that Everett Worthington recommends.

Write two letters, one stating your feelings and one from the other person's point of view. "Put yourself in his shoes," Worthington says of the other person. "Try to . . . understand why he may have said or done the things he did. Be specific. Explain his motives, thoughts, and feelings."[4]

You'll notice an important thing in the process.

"Forgiveness does not replace hurtful memories," Worthington explains. "It replaces the negative emotions attached to those memories."[5]

5

all the good-byes

{grieving the loss of what was}

If you have made mistakes, even serious ones, there is always another chance for you. What we call failure is not the falling down, but the staying down.

Mary Pickford

Two years into their marriage, Matthew and Sally were driving through their small town when Matthew became sullen.

"What's wrong?" Sally asked him.

"I was just thinking about Amelia [his daughter]. She didn't deserve to have her family broken up, and I still feel sad about it."

With a divorce comes a void, a deep sorrow for the loss of the dream of a family unscathed. It's normal to feel these effects long after the marriage has been dissolved. It's even normal to experience some of those feelings when in a new marriage. There are times when it's okay and normal to grieve the loss of what once was. You may not grieve the relationship or the person. You may grieve other things that you had in that relationship: the loss of the future, the history, the traditions, the friends, the memories, even the neighborhood.

Cheri missed her house. She and her first husband, Paul, had built a house together—her dream home. When the marriage fell apart, Cheri lost the house. Several years later, now remarried, Cheri and her new husband, Randy, bought a fixer-upper and began to rehab it. Since there were similarities in the work, Cheri occasionally brought up her first house.

"My husband would say, 'You wish you had that house, don't you?'" Cheri recalls. "I'd say, 'Yeah, I wish I had that house, but not with the person I built it with.' It was a wonderful house, but it had no love in it."

Jennifer missed the loss of all her childhood fantasies. By the time she and her husband divorced, she had already spent several years grieving the loss of her marriage. "I didn't feel the need to grieve the loss of my spouse," she says, "because I didn't have any feelings left for him. But I had so many dreams built up for my life, for my husband's life, and for our children's lives that were now all dead."

Jennifer and her first husband had married young, and she'd been filled with all the ideals of the "happily ever after" life. "I dreamed of the husband who worked 9:00 to 5:00 Monday through Friday, who was home every night being my companion, and who was an involved dad for the children. I dreamed about a nice God-centered home. I dreamed about happily adjusted children who never knew the pain of a broken home. I dreamed about hosting backyard barbeques for all our friends. They were all fantasies that never happened."

For years after her remarriage she continued to go through old photos and imagine the dreams they had—and "how those were left in ashes."

There are also the seemingly hidden emotional wounds that can pop open when we least expect or that we eventually learn to expect on special anniversaries.

In a *Marriage Partnership* article, "What I Wish I'd Known Before I Got Divorced," author and psychologist Georgia Shaffer writes about her friend Jan Coleman, who becomes depressed every Christmas. Jan told Georgia: "After twenty years the depression still hits me suddenly, without warning. I was first married in December, and my childhood sweetheart left me for another woman fifteen Decembers later. Every year I have a weepy week."[1]

Jan is fortunate that her second husband understands her need to grieve and gives her the space "to grieve again for the loss of that ideal family I spent my life imagining. . . . You're never free from the effects of that broken first marriage."[2]

grieving is normal

Because you've experienced a loss, you can expect to feel some of the effects of it. Psychologists agree that the grieving process is normal.

My husband, Scott, likens divorce to having your arm ripped out of its socket. I've heard stories of war victims who had an appendage blown off or amputated, and many times they will still try to scratch a foot or reach for something with an arm that isn't there.

That's kind of what happens in divorce. There's a part of you that's gone forever, a part of your soul that has been ripped from you. So you should grieve! You've lost an arm, as Scott would say.

Eileen's husband, Lee, had been divorced, and every once in a while Lee would become quiet and sad. When she'd ask him what was wrong, he mentioned that he was saddened by what he'd lost. "This was ten years later!" she says. "Then one day I was thinking about my grandmother who'd died in 1984. I could still become very sad about her passing. All of a sudden, God opened my eyes to what Lee was experiencing. I realized it's okay to mourn."

grieving is essential

Healing comes when we deal directly with our feelings and don't stuff them in some deep, dark part of our soul. When you feel sadness or other strong emotions wash over you, don't fight or suppress them. It's healthy and important to allow yourself to grieve your loss.

Carrie's husband left her January 15. For several years after the divorce—and even after her remarriage—on every January 15, Carrie would slip away to grieve. "It was the one time when I really allowed myself to mourn," she said. "I would cry over that marriage. I'm glad I did, because it freed me to give myself completely to my current husband."

To escape the pain of their aloneness, many times divorced individuals will become disconnected and never work through their grief process. These people skip grieving and walk into a new relationship with all the romance, affection, excitement, and newness. But, according to Christian therapist Shay Roop, "they have this huge pocket of pus, which is unresolved grief from their first relationship. That becomes a real issue in the second marriage, and will remain so until they deal with it."[3]

grieving the good

Obviously we won't grieve the bad parts of a marriage. When your spouse cheats on you, I'm sure you don't say, "Gee, I miss that period of my life. Never knowing if she's telling the truth. Never sure where she's been, or when she's coming home."

What we can, and do, miss are the good times.

Let's face it, 100 percent of your marriage wasn't bad. There must have been *some* good times, something funny you shared. Private jokes. A relaxing vacation. The first few years. When you first had children.

Those are the things to concentrate on.

66

grieving has no time limit

Scott and I were talking about this topic one afternoon recently, and he told me, "I may never be finished grieving. There may always be a part of me that will mourn the loss of what should have been mine."

Our society is uncomfortable with grieving. When someone dies, we hold a wake or visiting hours two or three days after the death, then we have the funeral. Then we expect the widow or widower to pick up and move on. It just doesn't happen that way.

Although deep grieving won't last forever, when we postpone it or rush through it, it lasts longer. I know a woman whose husband died more than five years ago. She still has everything of his in its place. She refuses to make any changes. Basically, because grieving brings pain to the surface, she refuses to grieve.

When we refuse to mourn, or deny that we even need to, that grief lingers painfully in the background and festers.

Allow yourself to feel sad. It's okay! Obviously, you don't want to wallow in it. But you can acknowledge those grief feelings.

By the end of Jennifer's first year of her second marriage, she felt she had finished grieving "the loss of the dreams for the little girl inside me." But it was at least another two or three years that she grieved the loss for her children as she watched them endure many difficult times of conflict between her and her ex-husband, going back and forth, being stuck in the middle of adult problems, and even telling her they wished she and their dad were back together. While it took time, eventually God began to heal Jennifer as she allowed herself the time to mourn.

your spouse grieves too!

I remember how surprised I was when I discovered I was mourning my loss in my marriage. I thought, *How can this be? I'm not the one divorced, my husband is.* But I realized I grieve for several things.

First, of course, I grieve for my husband and his loss. I love him and don't like to see him in pain. I see when he's feeling sad. I see the distress he carries because his daughter has lost a dream and innocence and security of an intact family. I try not to feel insecure, because I know he loves me, yet I realize our marriage wasn't his ideal. It has become that now. But it was not his first plan.

Second, I grieve for me.

In high school, I was crowned Miss Akron Teen and went on to become a finalist in the Ohio state pageant. But I didn't actually win the Miss Akron Teen pageant the night of the pageant. I won first runner-up.

Then, a month or so later, the dream came true. I received a phone call from a pageant representative who said the winner had relinquished her title and I was now the "it" girl. I became Miss Akron Teen.

I received the crown and all the privileges that came with it. Parades, photo ops, and a chance to go to the state pageant. Free modeling lessons. A college scholarship.

There was only one small problem: I never got to hear anybody announce my name as the winner. I never heard the applause. I never had the opportunity to walk down the runway, bearing the falling crown over my bouffant hair-sprayed coif, wearing the sliding Miss Akron Teen banner, holding the roses, doing the wave, throwing out kisses from my well-manicured hands, crying, and saying, "Oh, thank you! Thank you!" as I swooned.

Nope, I just received the phone call. The banner, crown, and trophy were mailed to me.

Whenever I talked about that pageant, I never mentioned that I was a winner by default. People knew me as the beauty pageant winner. And that's what counts in the end. But I know the truth: I was a runner-up.

So why am I reminiscing about my pageant days? Because I realized that pageant is the story of my marriage. I'm a runner-up wife. I'm not a "first" in my husband's life. I'm a "second." And, technically, I'll always be a second.

Yes, I get the crown and all the privileges: the parades, the photo ops, a great trophy husband. But I never got to experience the applause at being announced as the first.

His ex-wife experienced the "firsts" with him: first walk down the aisle, first love, first sexual experience, first house, first child, first promotion, first car, first gray hair. He has an entire history that doesn't include me. He knows people and has friends who know him in relation to his first wife.

And there are moments when I mourn that, when I mourn the loss of my dream to be "The First." While those times occur less and less frequently now, every once in a while that reality reemerges and reminds me of my loss.

the grieving process

How do we mourn our losses without wallowing? How do we mourn in a constructive, positive way?

Acknowledge your sadness over what you miss. "The biggest step for me was to recognize and admit what I was feeling," says Darla, who was married for ten years. Once she recognized and could name her feelings, she knew she could work through them.

Jennifer agrees: "Get honest and real. You figure out things as you go, and many things become clearer when looking at them from a distance."

There are two things that are key to healing. The first is, don't be afraid of pain. If we want to be healthy again, we have to face our pain. Facing the pain head-on isn't as bad as we fear it will be. Yes, it hurts—that's why it's called pain. But many people medicate their pain with work, business, alcohol, drugs, pornography, television, romance novels. The problem is that when the book is finished, or that hangover wears off, the pain is still there. The only way out of pain and into a life of freedom and healing is "through" it.

List your losses and lessons. When Christian therapists Shay and Robert Roop work with divorced and remarried couples, they focus on the grieving process. They ask their clients to write down the losses of the first marriage, such as lost security, trust, innocence. Then they discuss those losses. They've found it's important to discuss even the smallest losses.

"Typically, men don't understand grief as well as women," says Robert,

> so they get the basic loss of the relationship and pain of the divorce, the loss of finances, the loss of their children. They're not really able to recognize the loss of the sink where they used to shave, the routines of the day, the coming home to the kids. There are losses they haven't thought about, such as being able to walk in their house in the dark and find things. Old habits and patterns of living that they have to reestablish. Men aren't as adaptable as women, so it takes them longer to grieve.

When Lee and Eileen were dating, Lee mentioned that he missed having another person sleeping next to him. "It wasn't anything sexual," says Lee. "It was simply a warm body with whom to share the bed. It was a small, simple thing, and I missed that."

After writing out the list of losses, the Roops have their clients go back and write out the lessons from the losses. "I believe God is a God of compensation," says Shay. "He never allows us to go through a loss without giving us a lesson."

Try your own list and pray for God to show you the lessons of each item on your list. What can you learn? How can you apply that lesson to your current marriage?

Keep your grief from turning into guilt. Grief and guilt are two different emotions. Grieving is not saying, "Maybe if I only did this, then my marriage would have succeeded. If only . . ." Steer clear of those thoughts, since they don't help the healing process. They bring only more guilt and keep us stuck in the pain.

Take those thoughts captive by replacing them with other thoughts. Tell yourself that you refuse to think about those thoughts, and then concentrate on something else, something positive. "When I start to think guilt-inducing thoughts," says Jackie, "I think about what 2 Corinthians 5:17 says: 'If anyone is in Christ, he is a new creation; the old has gone, the new has come!'"

Steer clear of self-pity. When Jennifer would pull out her old photo albums, it became easy to fall into the self-pity trap. She noticed it more, though, when her children had pity parties. "Eventually, God nudged me to stop allowing my kids to focus on the loss of their dreams because it was leading to self-pity, which can be destructive—for both children and adults."

Jennifer began to focus on the positive with her children. "I reminded them that they have two sets of parents who love them so much they fight over them! They have two stable, loving homes. They get two sets of vacations, birthdays, and Christmas presents. Once we started to look at the positive aspects (as few and paltry as they may be), I saw that they became better at being positive."

Pray about it. Shelley would pray, "God, I'm feeling in a funk over my former marriage. Would you help me process this positively, help it not to affect my current marriage, and help me to put it in perspective, then move on?"

Give yourself time alone. When Jennifer went through her divorce, she spent many painful nights on her living room floor with the lights out, listening to worship music and crying out to God. "Each time I did that," she says, "a little more pain would slip out of my heart to be gone forever. The tears washed out my pain-polluted soul. Tears, feeling my pain, and time all healed me in the deep places that were crucial to my ever having a chance for a healthy relationship again."

Don't neglect your current marriage. While it's okay to feel sad, be careful not to allow your sadness to affect your current relationship.

"Sometimes I felt like a mistress to my husband," admits Sally. "He was so distraught over his ex-wife and how she left him that I didn't feel he was totally committed to me. He grieved, and grieved, and grieved, and left me alone."

Sally's marriage suffered a lot of stress and tension because her husband was unable to balance the grief with his new wife's needs.

If possible, talk about it. While Scott and I dated, I felt he talked about his past relationship a lot. There were times when I'd think, *Can we please move on? It's over already.* But he needed to process the experience. That was the best thing he could have done. Although it took a long time, talking placed the divorce in the open. It also helped me learn about him. The way his mind works, what to watch out for, what to avoid if I want to maintain his trust. His talking—incessantly, sometimes—turned out to be a good thing.

As Scott talked about his past with me he learned a lot about me too. He could trust me. I wasn't going to "tell" on him to the other side. I wasn't going to judge him. When Scott would talk about his past relationship, there were times when I was able to ask pointed questions about his actions in that marriage that helped him sift through the issues.

Talk with your spouse or a trusted friend or family member. Someone who will help guide your thoughts and who will ask the important questions. Remember that this is about cleaning house and being stronger and better as an individual and a spouse.

One caveat: when discussing your faults and grievances with your spouse, get it out in the open and then bury it. Both of you need to be up front and clear that these discussions and confessions will never be used as a weapon in an argument. Ever. Discuss the dirt, don't fling it.

Janie made the mistake of using something her husband had told her against him. "We were arguing, and I felt as though he was 'winning.' So I brought out the big guns and made a comment about how he was repeating what he did wrong in his first marriage. He exploded in anger and told me, 'If you ever wonder why I don't trust you or talk to you about my feelings, you remember this moment.' I felt horrible! But I couldn't take it back—even though I desperately wanted to."

Talk, but don't vomit. In other words, choose carefully what you say to your spouse, rather than spitting out everything you're feeling and thinking. Use some discretion. If your spouse is already feeling insecure over their place in your heart, it's important to make sure you're honest about what you are feeling, but it's also just as important to validate your mate.

Often it helps to say positive things about your current spouse before you spill the beans about the funk you're in. Rosa would tell Harry, "I love you. I love this marriage. I'm so glad I'm with you, and I appreciate how much you care about me. Right now, though, I'm feeling a little sad about my loss from my previous marriage. I'm just grieving a bit over the dream, not over the person. There's no reason for you to feel insecure or to feel as though you're less in my heart."

"While I'm glad she alerted me to what was going on inside her, it was difficult to hear," says Harry. "But the rational side of me understood. Honestly, I didn't want her to grieve at all! Yet I knew that was important for her to heal so she could eventually move on. I also realized that there would be a side of her that would be blocked from me forever. That's the unfortunate reality of divorce and remarriage."

Reach out to others. One of the best ways we can heal is to move outside our grief to help others who are in pain. Carol discovered that she was able to process and heal most when she started to teach a divorce recovery class.

There are many people who are in a similar place as you. Why not reach out to help them—and help yourself in the process?

helping your spouse grieve

Not long ago I shared with Scott about how I sometimes felt like the first runner-up in my beauty pageant. That was a vulnerable moment for me. I wondered, *What if I share this with him and he tells me I'm being overly sensitive or foolish? That I shouldn't feel this way?*

He listened quietly and nodded. Then he said the most healing thing to me. "You're right," he told me. "You're not the first. But you have something my first wife never had. You have my trust. You and I share a maturity, a respect, and a love that I was never able to have with her. That makes our marriage much more rich and blessed in my eyes. In that way, you are the first. You may not be the first in those other things, but you're the winner."

That's what counts in the end.

It's important that we allow each other to grieve. While we may not totally understand, and while we may not completely like it, when we allow our spouse to mourn honestly and openly, we allow them ultimately to draw nearer to us.

Sometimes, it helps just to listen. Sometimes it helps to touch a hand, an arm, a cheek. Ask your spouse how you can respond in a way that would be the most helpful. Your spouse will appreciate your concern and will be more open to you and the remarriage.

We don't need to feel threatened by the dips and valleys we or our mates go through. Again, the divorce was a death. It's only natural to, at times, mourn the loss. It doesn't mean we're mourning the spouse. We're mourning the loss, the significance, the meaning of what was supposed to be forever.

"I didn't want him to grieve because that meant he loved!" admits Sally. "I know it sounds selfish, but I wanted him to focus on me only and forget completely about his past." Eventually she discovered that if she allowed and encouraged her husband to mourn his loss and be honest about the pain, their marriage could actually be stronger.

"I can't believe that for so long in our marriage my insecurity actually caused Matthew not to heal," admits Sally. "That was wrong of me. I wish I had encouraged him long ago because we would be further along now in our marriage."

Try not to be reluctant to hear your spouse grieve. Your reluctance will only stop them from grieving. And the depths of their emotions will stay frozen and stuck, which means the emotions won't be available to you either. Instead, think about the apostle Paul's words: "Love is patient, love is kind. It does not envy. . . . When I was a child, I talked like a child, I thought like a child, I reasoned like a child. When I became a man, I put childish ways behind me" (1 Corinthians 13:4, 11).

Do yourself and your marriage a favor. Don't be afraid of hurting. It will get better if you allow yourself and your spouse to feel the pain.

for *even* after

Sometimes men don't want to grieve their loss. They get stuck in denial and are afraid to feel anything because typically it can move into anger. Denial and anger are the first two stages of normal grieving.

A husband dealing with that can move closer into mourning with this help: start talking about things that tap into his emotions. Christian therapist Shay Roop suggests starting the conversation with a word picture.

For instance, you could say, "You know, honey, one of the things I miss most is that old antique mirror hanging over the sink. I sort of miss doing my hair in that mirror every morning. Do you ever feel like that?" Or you could say, "It must be difficult for you to come home and not be greeted by your children. It must be hard just to see the dog."

This has nothing to do with the ex-spouse. What you want is to tap gently into that frozen lake of grief, to be empathetic.

6

oh, lonesome, loser me

{dealing with the stigma of divorce and remarriage}

> I never really address myself to any image anybody
> has of me. That's like fighting with ghosts.
>
> Sally Field, actress

Greg was devastated when his wife filed for divorce. His wife had
had an affair with a co-worker and wanted out of the marriage
so she could wed her lover. The divorce was an ugly court battle
over child custody and divvying up the couple's assets.

"I was crushed through the entire process," says Greg. "The one
place I thought I could find comfort, the church, ended up being
the place where I felt least accepted. People wouldn't talk to me
or even look at me. It was as if I had some contagious disease."

So many times, we feel the stigma of the "divorce" label—even
long after we've been remarried. I love those forms you fill out
where you have to list gender, then you have to mark the marital
status. The list usually includes: single, married once, divorced
and remarried. They never let you forget! You've been tagged!

Our culture, and even some of our churches, stigmatize failure. We go to church, and people don't talk with us anymore. Some may hint that we're no longer Christians, or never really were. They subtly say, "If you fail at anything, you are incompetent, a loser, and certainly not a Christian. What is wrong with you?" Many Christians are confused about how they should respond to the "losers." Obviously, not all Christians who have trouble dealing with divorced people are operating out of mean-spiritedness. Many are simply confused or uncertain about how to act. But let's face it—sometimes people who call themselves Christians can be brutal. I've met some real tough birds who claimed to be Christian, then acted anything but. "Well-intentioned" comments that came out scathing. It can hurt, can't it?

Darla dealt with painful comments from her future mother-in-law. "Before my husband and I were married, I overheard my future mother-in-law comment to my fiancé, 'She's used goods. Why do you want her? You deserve so much better.'"

Gina received the comments from church friends. They told her, "Wow, he certainly has the baggage, huh?"

"That stung!" Gina says. "I know they didn't mean to hurt me. They were thoughtless in what they said. But it made me feel horrible—not only for me but also for what I felt they knew about my husband."

In his book *Grace and Divorce*, Les Carter sums it up well.

> Most . . . Christian divorcees are conflicted. They want to move forward in the confidence that they can continue to be useful to God. However, they are haunted by the nagging guilt that they have contradicted the laws of Christianity in order to move from disaster toward healthiness. A high percentage of these people realize that they have not been able to follow God's perfect plan, but because of the queasiness of some fellow Christians they carry the extra burden of feeling that they must prove themselves at their most emotionally depleted time.[1]

Carol lost a church speaking engagement because they found out she was divorced and remarried. "Ministry doors have been slammed shut to me because of my divorce," she admits. "And some of them will never be opened."

Eventually, we even buy into that mind-set. We feel like failures, as though we're not good enough, that we don't measure up, that we're second-class Christians. We carry around the "loser" label like Hester Prynne wore the scarlet A in *The Scarlet Letter*.

"Every time I drop off my daughter at her dad's, I am reminded of my failures," says Tracie. "I've let somebody down. That's a tough pill to swallow."

Cheri remembers that she was in such disbelief that she could have another opportunity to marry, that she thought, *There's going to be something that will go wrong!*

This "loser" label can even apply to someone who's married to a divorced person. Eileen dealt with this—especially when she'd mention her husband was divorced. She found herself quickly defending him by saying, "But it was a biblical divorce." Or she'd say, "There was adultery involved. Multiple times." (As though once wasn't bad enough!)

"Honestly," she admits, "there are still moments when I blurt out those 'justifiers.' There's a part of me that wants to make sure people don't judge my husband for whatever reason. But also, there's a part of me that doesn't want people to judge *me*. It's selfish, I know, but I don't want people to think that I'm an adulterer! And I don't want people to think my husband has problems."

Sally even dealt with the stigma she directed toward her own husband. "There would be times when I'd have to fight myself to keep from thinking, *What's wrong with him that he couldn't stay married?*"

Kevin struggled with labeling his wife before they were married. "I was hesitant to marry her because of her past. When we met, I was a thirty-two-year-old virgin. I'd saved myself for a special woman whom I believed would have saved herself for me. I never imagined that I'd find myself in a relationship with a divorced mother of two children."

loser no longer!

In the previous four chapters we've dealt with our part in the death of our marriages, seeking forgiveness from God, giving forgiveness to others, and mourning our losses. Now it's time to move forward.

If God is a God who takes our sins and remembers them no more (Isaiah 43:25), then we are not losers. We no longer have to live under the stigma of failure. We have been forgiven, and we are free.

May I get an "Amen"?

Let's lose the loser label, shall we?

what God thinks about you

Jennifer dealt with the shame factor after her divorce and even into her new marriage. "I felt ashamed and could hardly look people in the eye." Even her ex-husband contributed to her shame. "But God used my ex-husband's graceless and condemning words to drive me to find out what God thought of me." This is what she discovered: "There is now no condemnation for those who are in Christ Jesus" (Romans 8:1).

God's grace became a huge reality to Jennifer because for the first time, she recognized her need for it. For so long she felt she didn't deserve God's forgiveness and grace. "My heart was so broken. But when I really read those words from Romans, it was as if I felt God tell me, 'Because of what my Son did for you, you are no longer guilty.' That was incredibly freeing for me."

Jennifer says that since the experience, she no longer allows herself to be aware of other people's comments. "Now I don't care what people think about my past. I am who I am today because of my past, not in spite of it. I am willing to talk about my past with confidence based on what God has done to redeem my life and to restore my dreams."

She also finds it has worked wonders in her remarriage. "My husband dealt with my 'stigma.' Over time, though, his fears about my baggage subsided as he realized I am the woman I am today *because of my past.* He could see many areas of growth in me because of my divorce, and he loves the ways my character has grown."

Take a look at some other things God thinks about you.

"The LORD will fulfill his purpose for me; your love, O LORD, endures forever—do not abandon the works of your hands" (Psalm 138:8).

"Call to me and I will answer you . . . I will bring health and healing" (Jeremiah 33:3, 6).

"We know that in *all things* God works for the good of those who love him, who have been called according to his purpose" (Romans 8:28, italics added).

"If anyone is in Christ, he is a new creation; the old has gone, the new has come!" (2 Corinthians 5:17).

We have a God whose mercies are new to us every day. He gives us freedom to make our choices. While they may not be the right choices, if we go to him with a pure and honest heart and admit where we failed, he will forgive us. More than anything else, he wants a relationship with us. When he forgives, he totally forgets.

how to live in grace

Knowing God forgives and forgets is the best start for leaving the loser stigma behind. Other reminders help too . . .

Realize everybody has a skeleton or two—or twelve—in their closet. We're all losers. Sorry to be politically incorrect in our world of helping people's self-esteem, but this is the truth. Apart from Christ, we are all losers.

Many people like to qualify or prioritize sins and mistakes. White-collar crimes aren't as bad as other types. What Martha Stewart did to land in jail wasn't as bad as robbing a bank or mugging a little old lady on a street corner. Lying to my boss about being ill isn't as bad as committing adultery.

I'm not convinced there are levels of sin. If God is holy, then even the smallest, most insignificant sin puts a chasm between us. And a chasm is still a chasm. How wide or narrow the chasm doesn't matter, because we still need Jesus to bridge it! The apostle Paul writes, "For all have sinned and fall short of the glory of God" (Romans 3:23). It isn't "some have sinned" or "most have sinned" or "sinners have sinned, but not Christians." It doesn't read, "For all have sinned and fall short of the glory of God—especially divorced people." All of us are guilty. The sins may be different, but the results are exactly the same—we've fallen short of God's perfect standard.

Whenever I start to have an attack of the insecurities, I do an experiment. Wherever I am—whether it's at work, at church, in the grocery store line—I look around and really start to study people. I try to find the best dressed, the most "put together" person, and I think, *That person is a screwup.*

Okay, I don't really think that. But I do realize that the most "put together" people need God just as desperately as I do. We all have dysfunctions.

Several years ago a popular book titled *I'm Okay, You're Okay* hit the market. I think the more appropriate title should have been *I'm Not Okay and Neither Are You.*

Julie puts it another way, "If people have a problem with me or with my past, they need to find someone else who can fit into their illusions of squeaky clean Christianity, because life isn't like that."

Everybody needs grace. We all need a Savior, even those people fortunate enough not to have experienced a divorce.

Steer clear of folks who don't "get it." It doesn't matter what you do or say, there will be some people who just won't ever get it.

One evening when I finally decided to become vulnerable in my small group, I explained that my agreement to live in the house my husband had shared with his ex-wife turned out to be a bad decision. I said, "I'm trying to be patient, but it's difficult. And I just keep holding out until I can have a house that is mine."

One woman, who had never been divorced or remarried, reprimanded me for my selfishness and told me—in front of the group—that she was concerned about how I was treading into dangerous waters over what I perceived as "mine."

I sat in shock.

Afterward, several people approached me and apologized for what this woman had said. "She has no idea what she's talking about. She's never been in your shoes," they told me. But it was too late; the damage was done, and that evening I chose not to share vulnerably with that group again.

I forgave her, not because I particularly wanted to, but because I understood she was speaking out of ignorance. I prayed for her and tried to be respectful during the times I saw her, but in the future I tried to steer clear of her as much as possible. Especially as I watched her consistently say ignorant things to other people in our group.

Why put yourself through undue stress around people who will be toxic to your spirit? Just say no. Sometimes that may mean staying away from Thanksgiving dinners or family outings or certain church functions. I'm not suggesting we run away. Of course, try to give these people the benefit of the doubt, because maybe they simply don't realize how hurtful their words can be. But above all, I'm suggesting we protect ourselves from people who are ignorant or hateful on purpose, who open their mouths and prove they are clueless.

There's no need to hang around people who either put you down or give you a false sense of identity.

Protect yourself. This includes your mind. The enemy would love nothing better than to chip away at your self-esteem, telling you, "Everybody is judging you. God has judged you and it's over. You're a loser. So give it up."

A great way to close your mind to those thoughts is to pray God's Word back to him. Pray the Bible by reciting Scriptures you remember.

I've noticed huge differences in my days when on my way to work I pray, "God, help me to take captive every thought to make it obedient to Christ" (2 Corinthians 10:5, NLT).

We're not responsible for what others say, think, or do to us. If Darla's mother-in-law wants to say hurtful things about Darla and her past, there is absolutely nothing Darla can do to control that. And Darla is not accountable for her mother-in-law's behavior. What Darla is accountable for, what she can control, is her own thoughts, words, and actions.

When someone hurts us, we don't balance the playing field by retaliating in kind. That only serves to fuel the problem and keep everything off-kilter. When those thoughts enter your mind that you know aren't God-honoring, whether they are toward yourself or toward others, pray, "God, take my thoughts captive. Help me to concentrate on thoughts that bring you pleasure."

There's a time to talk and a time to clam up. You'll never be able to handle pushing off people's comments or attitudes until your soul is clean. Once you understand who you are in Christ, that you've been forgiven, then you are better able to handle outside forces.

My problem often comes when I've been pushed and pushed and pushed—then it's *watch out!* But that's not what God desires.

When we confront, we need to pray first. It's better to keep quiet at the time of the offense, to think about what that person said, then work through your thoughts and feelings before commenting.

So, when in doubt, don't blurt it out. Things said are impossible to take back.

When you must confront, do so in love—not in the way that makes us feel great right at the moment. There's a thing called tact, after all. Remember, we're responsible for what we say. It's best to say, "I've been dealing with an issue, and I'd like to talk with you about it. I felt [fill in the blank here—hurt, misunderstood, judged, sad] when I heard some comments made about my past. I'm sure you didn't mean to say anything that would cause me such pain. I just wanted to let you know how that made me feel."

Now let go of those negative emotions—and any frustration with the person who spurred them.

People may be horrified by what they've done. They may even apologize. Great. If not—if they say, "Yeah, what of it?"—you probably shouldn't expect an apology. But that's their deal. God sees the interactions; he takes notice, and he will make things right.

After you've brought up the offense, if the offender doesn't see the error of his or her ways, don't try to beat that dead horse—or even kill the horse so you can beat it. Understand that some people simply will not be able to give you what you need, namely understanding and respect. Consider the source. Be okay in the fact that you're not accountable for that person's behavior. Then treat the offender with kindness.

Reconnect with family and friends. Surround yourself with people who know your journey and hold you accountable. These are the close friends with whom you can tell your struggles and share your spiritual journey.

Realize God isn't finished with you yet. One of my favorite verses in the Bible is the oft-quoted passage from Jeremiah 29:11 that says, "I have a plan for you—to comfort you and to give you a hope and a future." I love this verse because it doesn't have a disclaimer. Jeremiah doesn't say, "I had a plan for you, but you went and screwed it up, so now you're on your own."

Think about this. Jeremiah was quoting God and talking to the Israelites. Talk about God's chosen screwed-up folks. They were forever messing up. They were constantly sinning against God and breaking their covenants with him. They committed "adultery" against him more times than we can count. But there stood God, talking through his prophet Jeremiah, saying, "I have a plan for you, and it includes great things!"

Remember that Jeremiah 29:11 still applies to us. "I have a plan for you—to comfort you and to give you a hope and a future." That now includes your spouse. God has a plan for your marriage.

Now. Today. And it doesn't include living under a loser status. It includes getting right with God in the spiritual department. It includes a hunk of forgiveness. It includes a powerful ministry that you can have.

Take your failures and let God use them. While it wasn't his plan for you to divorce, God isn't stumped by our choices. He can take the ugly mess of our lives and turn it into something beautiful—despite us!

I look at my relationship with Scott and I know God brought us together. It wasn't God's plan for Scott's first wife to leave the marriage and her family. Yet God took the pain of her wrong choices and brought beautiful things from it. I can't explain it; that's the mystery of our faith.

But when God does something beautiful in our lives—and he's done it in everyone's, including yours—he expects something in return. We can take our life story, our experiences, and use them to help others who are hurting as we once were.

That's what Jennifer did; she now talks openly about her and her ex-husband's affairs, subsequent divorce, and God's immense grace. "God has given me so much to be grateful for—even after I caused him and my family so much pain! My ex-husband and I can't redo or undo the past. That pain will always be there. But I can help others who admit they need help, just like I do. Jesus didn't come for the healthy (Matthew 9:12). He came to help the sick. Those are the real people who understand human nature and realize just how frail they are. Revelation 12:11 says, 'They overcame him [Satan] by the blood of the Lamb and by the word of their testimony.' This is my testimony—how bad, sinful, and needy I was before Christ and what he did to make me into a whole and redeemed person. If someone has a problem with that, they have a problem with the gospel of Jesus Christ."

Carmen agrees. "I will be true to who I am in Christ," she says. "I will not cover up my past or try to hide or erase it. That may cost me some ministry opportunities, but I won't lie. I think God honors that. God can use the pain in my life for good."

In 1 Timothy 1:15–17, the apostle Paul writes:

86

Here is a trustworthy saying that deserves full acceptance: Christ Jesus came into the world to save sinners—of whom I am the worst. But for that very reason I was shown mercy so that in me, the worst of sinners, Christ Jesus might display his unlimited patience as an example for those who would believe on him and receive eternal life. Now to the King eternal, immortal, invisible, the only God, be honor and glory for ever and ever. Amen.

Amen, indeed.

for *even* after

Former First Lady Eleanor Roosevelt said she overcame her lack of "looks" and "smarts" with courage. "No one can make you feel inferior without your consent," she was often quoted as saying.

She's right. You can deflect those "loser" feelings with the courage of kindness—kindness to others and to yourself.

There's a proverb that says we gather more flies with honey than with vinegar. Repaying hurt with kind words and actions is a great torture plan: our enemies expect us to retaliate in kind. When we don't, it really fries them! The writer of Proverbs says, "If your enemy is hungry, give him food to eat; if he is thirsty, give him water to drink. In doing this, you will heap burning coals on his head, and the LORD will reward you" (25:21–22).

In other words, repay pain with kindness. Remember, "the Lord will repay him [or her] for what he has done" (2 Timothy 4:14).

part 2

fields of schemes

navigating a way with all the others

The only difference between death and divorce is that in
divorce you have to keep dealing with the corpse.

UNKNOWN

7

the ex factor

{throttling is not an option}

People who fight fire with fire usually end up with ashes.

Abigail Van Buren, better known as Dear Abby

Eileen remembers the first time she met her husband's ex-wife. It was at a graduation party, and the ex expertly set the stage for how she would handle Eileen and Lee's relationship: she butted in.

"I wish no harm to come to this woman," says Eileen. "What I wish is that she would simply disappear from our lives. That she would, in fact, 'get a life.' But she seems intent on 'getting *my* life.'"

When Eileen and Lee decided to move to a neighboring community, they were excited about the possibility of starting from scratch, where no one would know their business, where no one would know them—or better, where no one would know the ex.

"Imagine our surprise," she says, "when our old neighbors came to our house as we were packing and began to spout off information about our new house, where it was located, what it looked like, and when we were moving. Since we had shared this information with none of them, we asked our neighbors the same question: 'How did you know?' Each answer was the same: 'Linda told me.' Come to find out, Linda had been insinuating to our friends and neighbors that we were all good friends, so she could get more information about us!"

Lily had a similar experience. Over coffee one day, she told me, "My marriage would be fantastic but for the eternal, omnipresent ex-wife. She constantly calls my husband and wants to 'get together.' She attends our church (it's a church of more than ten thousand people) and sits close to us, then 'greets' *me* after the service with a hug and kiss. She drives by our house. She does everything possible to make us believe she is psycho. It's working."

They say when you marry, you also marry your spouse's family. Here's a news flash: if your spouse has children, not only do you marry the family, but you also marry his or her ex. For your entire life. And there will most likely be times when the ex would like nothing better than to make sure your marriage is miserable. It's in the job description, or something.

Even if you get along well with your ex, that doesn't mean your new mate will be touchy-feely about that person. Jealousy, comparisons, and insecurities can all play into a new marriage. These are especially important times for us to remain united as husband and wife against the outside disruptions of the ex, who often can wield manipulations, guilt, demands, and lies like a professional.

don't drive the wedge!

There have been many cases in which the ex "pops" in just long enough to disrupt harmony, then retreats into the shadows to watch his or her handiwork. The problem is that instead of focusing on the ex, some couples turn the ex's actions on their marriage and drive a wedge between each other. Truth factor: the ex isn't worth it.

Repeat this with me (as often as necessary): no matter what, the ex isn't worth it. The ex is not worth any disconnect in my marriage. Period. End of subject.

Our loyalty is to our spouse.

I've seen this happen over and over, where the ex-mate uses the children as pawns. The ex will use their history as parents to cause trouble in the new marriage. Please, just don't go there. Don't slide down to that person's level. I understand that you'd really like to throttle the person, then ship him or her to a work camp in the Guadalcanal. The reality is, if you have children, your ex is here to stay. So since the Guadalcanal thing is a no-go, and throttling could land you in court, there must be some better ways to handle the situation.

In situations in which the ex is a negative factor, the name of the game is about power and control: who has it, who wants it, and who will do anything to gain it. There are some rules to this game:

1. I cannot change the ex, nor can I control him/her.
2. He/she may not play fair.
3. I can give him/her power and control to win the game.
4. Number 3 is not an option.

It took Sally some time to figure out the rules, but she finally won. "It took me a long time to get to the point where I could say her name or even think about her without seeing her strung up by her toenails. Imaginary arrows were flung. Impressive imaginary conversations were had—in which I gave her a part of my brilliant mind with profound and witty comebacks of what I thought of her," says Sally. "There are few people I can honestly say I truly and profoundly dislike. She was one of them. And she did nothing to take herself from the list."

"What happened?" I asked.

"Eventually, God stepped rudely into my mind during those imaginary throttling sessions and started to replace them with kinder thoughts. Not that I have a desire to go shopping with her or have our families take vacations together anytime soon. But anger toward her and her actions is no longer there. Incredulity, yes. Pity, often. But not anger."

unraveling the rules

Take a closer look at those "rules," and you'll find some gems for living.

1. I cannot change the ex, nor can I control him/her. The ex-husband persists in calling to discuss more than just your child. The ex-wife makes financial demands that supersede earlier agreements. He disrupts your time together as a family. She has access to your husband's time, attention, and finances. He exerts his power over visitation rights, times, and places. She threatens to sue him if her demands are not met. He confronts you in public. She interrupts you and your mate during a romantic dinner date. He turns the children against you.

I had a friend who recently died from cancer. Several weeks before his death, he argued with his ex-wife over where she would sit at his funeral—she felt she should sit in the front row; he felt she should not even be present. A few days before his death, his ex-wife sued him for child support and demanded more of his life insurance money because she had just started an addition to her house.

That's low.

2. He/she may not play fair. Over the years, Jennifer's children have been the rope in a game of tug-of-war. "My ex would like to cause pain to me any way he can," says Jennifer. "The kids are the only tool he has to use. I often end up losing the battle willingly in order to protect the girls because he doesn't think how his actions hurt them too." Recently, her children invited her to their school's open house. When she arrived, her kids stayed close to their father and wouldn't say hello or acknowledge her presence.

She left early because she knew her children had been put in an awkward position. So to relieve their stress, she left. "The sad thing is," she says, "that many times he has driven a wedge between me and the children with his tactics, making me look bad in ways I don't discover until later. By then I am helpless to do anything about it."

Janie struggles with her husband's ex when the ex tries to tell Janie how to parent. "She treats me as though I don't know how to care for the children. So she'll say rude things about me in front of them."

The ex may use the children as spies to dig up "dirt" in your marriage. One wife admitted that she continued to have her mail sent to her ex-husband's house—even after he remarried and moved.

You may be surprised that the ex doesn't play life by the golden rule. Don't be. Expect it. Then if and when she does, you can be pleasantly surprised.

3. I can give him/her power and control to win the game. When you don't set boundaries with the ex or even with the stepchildren, he gains control. When you get into a tit-for-tat match with him, he wins. He gets the pleasure of seeing that he can make you react.

Early in her new marriage, Brenda's ex-husband spread rumors that he and Brenda were secretly still involved and were getting back together. "I wanted to tell him what I thought of him," admits her husband, Evan. "But I had to be above that. It would only add to the problem. I didn't want him to think he was getting to me."

The ex is usually looking for any signs that the remarriage is in trouble. Don't give her that pleasure. Don't let the ex know that anything she has said or done has ruffled feathers in your marriage. On the positive side, in her book *Ex-Wives and Ex-Lives*, Paula Egner believes, "You may be surprised to discover that becoming a *next-wife* has forged you into being one of the most creative, resilient, thick-skinned women on this planet."[1] Make that work for you to win the game. Also, Paula continues,

If your gut clenches when he tells you that she's called him yet again at work to discuss some trivial matter, trust your *instincts*—

not her. But she divorced him, you say! If she'd have wanted him, she would have kept him! Tsk, tsk. . . . The issue isn't whether or not she wanted him, it's that now you could replace her forever in his life. Don't be naïve. Even if she doesn't want to remarry him, that doesn't mean she's going to sit idly by and watch him be happy with another woman.[2]

4. Number 3 is not an option. Make the ex a non-issue. Be the bigger person—no matter how your ex treats you.

respect for your ex

Be the bigger person? Easier said than done? Well, there are ways to help you treat your ex better than you feel you're being treated. Try these things:

Pray for that person. You knew this one was coming, didn't you? Honestly, this is my least favorite. Because I know when I pray about something I have to have the right attitude. That means I have to pray about me *first*.

The predicament is that often when the ex has shown up on the scene, I'd rather pray like King David in Psalms: "Strike all my enemies on the jaw; break the teeth of the wicked" (3:7, NLT); "Break the arm of the wicked and evil man; call him to account for his wickedness that would not be found out" (10:15, NLT); "Brandish spear and javelin against those who pursue me . . . may those . . . be disgraced and put to shame; may those who plot my ruin be turned back in dismay. . . . May their path be dark and slippery, with the angel of the LORD pursuing them. . . . May ruin overtake them by surprise. . . . Then my soul will rejoice in the LORD and delight in his salvation" (35:3–4, 6, 8–9, NLT).

Unfortunately, I don't think that's the smartest choice. It's a stretch, I realize. Asking God to rain down tar and feathers may feel good at first, but it probably isn't the most appropriate course of action.

Instead, Jesus asks us to pray this way: "Pray for your enemies. Bless those who curse you" (Matthew 5:44). So, there you have it.

We ask God to bless them. If for no other reason than, if you have children, that person is the parent to your child or stepchild. Pray that they would make wise parenting decisions. Pray that they would be open to hearing God's voice. That God would be free to work in that person's life. (Pray that the ex would miraculously receive a big, fat raise and promotion that includes a relocation to Taiwan.) Pray that, gulp, your heart would be softened toward them—simply because you know God loves them and created them in his image.

I've found that when I pray for Scott's ex-wife, my kinder feelings toward her grow. I allow God the freedom to work in my mind and heart to accomplish what he wants in that relationship and in my life.

I tend to act better toward her when I've prayed for and about her. I can't explain it; I just know it works. But it's not just the quickie prayers. Sometimes, it's serious, time-investing prayers. Sometimes it's the fasting prayers. It's an investment. But if you're stuck with that person in your life, for the rest of your life, the prayer investment is definitely worth it.

Avoid the comparison trap. Some women, especially, are concerned with outdoing their husband's ex-wife, succumbing to jealousy when they feel they don't measure up, and being condescending when they feel they do.

One wife, Emma, says, "Of course, I hope my marriage is healthier than his first one. But it isn't about whether I'm a better person than she is."

Comparisons between your first marriage and your current one sidestep the real issues. If you're feeling insecure about the ex, deal with that head-on. Acknowledge your insecurities, pray about them, journal them, but don't allow them to overtake your sanity or your rational thought. Allowing comparisons to overtake your brain can devastate your marriage. And what's our motto? The ex isn't worth it.

More than likely, your spouse is not comparing you to his ex. And if he is, that's his deal, not yours. You deal with what you can change.

There are moments when I'll have misleading thoughts: *Did Scott's ex-wife do this better? Does Scott compare me to her?*

It makes a difference for Scott to tell me, "I never had this in my previous marriage. I never felt this with her like I do with you. I've never had a reason to doubt my trust in you. With her I doubted it from the moment we were married."

Believe your spouse when he tells you these things. Give him the benefit of the doubt!

Don't allow yourself to think, *Is there still a part of him that loves her?* That's where the verse about taking captive your thoughts, to make them obedient to Christ, comes into play. Take those thoughts captive.

Sarah had to deal with the weight issue. "Troy's ex-wife is thin and stylish. I'm not," she says. "I'm low maintenance, not super thin, and not stylish. His ex spent a lot of money on clothing and the whole thing. If I let down my guard, there are moments when I can find myself thinking, *Does he wish I were thinner? Does he wish I were more of a 'trophy' wife?*"

I received a letter at *Marriage Partnership* last year about comparisons. Here's what this second wife had to say: "The ghost of the first, as I call her, is at best only an annoyance, at worst a hurricane wreaking total destruction. At times, I believe she is living in the house with us. I will be discussing a problem or situation in our life, and my husband will proceed to tell me exactly how he handled it during his previous marriage. I sometimes find myself wondering why he thinks I would care how they handled the situation. Once I even asked him why he thought doing the same thing over was a good idea since that solution did not work the first time."

Establish clear, firm boundaries. Limit conversations to those matters that deal with the present and with the children. Let an attorney or mediator settle all other concerns. If the ex wants to move out of bounds, then feel free to walk away or hang up on conversations that stray into other business. Any leeway opens the door for more difficulties. Say, "I'm not interested in discussing this. Let's try again later when we can focus on the schedule." Then, politely hang up the phone or walk away.

Tell your ex from the outset that any conversations will be limited to important issues about the children and nothing else.

"I told my ex that if she brought up any other issues, I would warn her then hang up," says Dan. "She thought I was lying. So the next time she called and started an argument, I told her I wasn't going to discuss the topics she wanted. When she wouldn't drop it, I said, 'I'm hanging up the phone now.' And I did."

With each conversation, alert your current spouse to what happened and when. Scott tells me each time his ex-wife calls and exactly what she says. He asks me to listen to each phone message she leaves on his cell phone. That grows our trust and love because I know he respects me and keeps no secrets.

Your blended family's business is, and should remain, private. This has been an issue that Eileen and Lee have had to deal with. Lee's ex-wife would regularly contact them or some other member of his family or use his daughter to find out the scoop on their private life. Recently she called to talk to Lee. When Eileen answered the phone, the ex sidestepped why she called. "I asked her what she wanted, and she said, 'You sound upset. Are you and Lee having marital problems?' That was the end of the conversation. But then she called back and left a long message on our answering machine about my marriage!"

One couple had to go so far as to threaten to file a harassment report with the police if the ex-wife didn't stop her behavior. Just be sure to follow through on the boundaries issues with clear consequences.

Respect your spouse's wishes. Clark used to feel attacked from all sides: his ex-wife regularly called to renew old arguments, and Emily, angry at how he handled the situation, would be critical of him. "I always felt as though Emily thought I was a coward," he says.

One day, however, Emily calmly told Clark how his conversations with his ex were hurting their marriage because he chose to spend their family time yelling at his ex. "I finally understood that she just wanted things to be better in our home."

If your spouse is feeling insecure or frustrated by your ex-mate's actions, it's better to err on your spouse's side. That doesn't give anyone carte blanche to act in a hurtful way, but if your spouse asks you not to spend time alone with your ex, for instance, then respect that wish.

Several years ago Hillary wrote to me in response to an article she'd read in *Marriage Partnership* about handling the angry ex. Here's what she had to say: "My husband permitted things to go on for too many years before he could see the destruction his first wife was instigating. It nearly cost us our family. Men need to listen to their wives with an open mind. I am thankful that we have survived, but my trust had been destroyed, and though I trust more now than seven years ago, the experience will weigh on me probably the rest of my life."

practice forgiveness

For years, Scott and I struggled with anger toward his ex-wife. We would just get to the point where we felt we could forgive her, and then she would pop back into our lives, overstepping boundaries to cause trouble, even after my husband's daughter became an adult. Each time, the forgiveness would be a little more difficult. To the point where I'd think, *If this woman doesn't remove herself from my marriage, I'm going to explode.*

I've had to work hard at forgiving her. Yet I know that's what pleases God. When I don't forgive her, she wins. I allow her to control my emotions and attitudes. I even allow her to control my conversations with my husband. Scott and I joke that he doesn't have feelings for her; he has feelings about her. But what's our motto? The ex isn't worth harming our marriage.

Scott and I will probably always have to deal with continually forgiving her. We understand Peter's question to Jesus: "How many times, Lord, must I forgive?" Jesus said, "Seventy times seven" (Matthew 18:21–22). Okay, if you want to get technical, that is 490 times. Don't think we haven't considered buying a notebook to keep track! But somehow I think that's probably not what Jesus meant.

It may be difficult to pray, "God help me to love her," because frankly, that may be too huge a step. But we can pray, "God, help me to pity her." Pity brings us closer to forgiveness.

it's not about me

While sometimes it feels personal, it's important to remember the ex's actions and words truly are not about you. If the ex is acting out his frustrations, having temper tantrums, acting the part of an imp, the thing to remember is that the ex would do that to *any* new spouse. It's about the new position you hold.

Expect that he may blame you for everything bad in his life. Expect that he may pit his kids against you. Expect that he may start the rumor mill, or any number of other things. Many exes may not love their former mate, but they sure don't want anyone else to either.

Eileen felt as though her husband's ex wanted her husband to pine away, lovelorn. "She couldn't stand it when he no longer grieved his loss!" she says. "She didn't want him, but she didn't want him not to want her. She did everything she could to disrupt the wedding and our marriage. She showed up at our house and would just walk in. She'd say inappropriate things to me about my husband. It was unbelievable!"

Eileen realized it really had nothing to do with her. "The ex has issues that she and God need to work out. She uses me to keep from dealing with the truth in her own life. The realization helped me pity her and not take things personally. That also helped me to respond more nicely, rather than seethe inside. Now I just think, *This is all so about her, not me.*"

for *even* after

If the ex is determined to play things his or her way, here are several options:

Talk to a good attorney or mediator to find out your rights and then do all your communication through that person.

Use email or letters only. This has multiple advantages, allowing you to draft and redraft your thoughts until your letter has proper tone and substance. You'll have a chance to review the content with your spouse before sending it. A written note minimizes the risk of the ex misunderstanding what you are communicating and also gives you a written record of what is said to refer to later if need be.

To work out scheduling issues because of the children, check out OurFamilyWizard.com. This site is recommended and used by divorced parents to share calendars, records, contacts, and expense logs with ex-spouses. The site offers tools that enable divorced parents to share scheduling, medical, school, sports, and cost-splitting information about their children, for ninety-nine dollars a year per parent.

Make specific requests regarding visitation or mutual co-parenting responsibilities, which will help avoid many potential misunderstandings and conflicts. Write your requests in clear, concise language. Run them by your current spouse.

Always pray and prepare for discussions with your ex-spouse.

8

the stepparent trap
{how to manage a marriage and "bonus" children}

You can shake us up and we blend really well for
moments, days, months even. After a while, though,
we have a tendency to settle back into original family
lines and loyalties.

Natalie Nichols Gillespie

Ah, children. Those little masters of manipulation and divisiveness. Children, by their very nature, are self-centered. (Aren't we all?) They are not interested in your love life. They are not interested in your happiness. They are not interested in the success of your remarriage. They are interested primarily—no, not primarily—entirely in their own well-being.

Yes, my friend, I am a stepmother.

Why doesn't Disney ever do an animated flick about a *kind, good-natured* stepmother who falls in love with her handsome prince—who, besides being a prince, is also the father of several lovely children who delight in nothing less than making their stepmother's life miserable.

No, Disney portrays stepmothers as wicked.

Many remarried folks are concerned about being the best step-parents they can possibly be, and they take their new role seriously. Some really do want to have great relationships with their stepkids. I'm a stepmother who truly likes my stepdaughter. I think she has great potential. She's smart, funny, pretty, and truly a lovely young lady.

But we struggled with the adjustment period, and my marriage took some hits. Studies have shown that most remarriage struggles are over stepchildren. My husband and I were no exception. While Scott and I didn't argue often, when we did, it was over the ex or some parenting issue. I was new to the gig and struggling to find my place in Scott's and his daughter's lives. And frankly, many times I didn't handle it so well.

When I really contemplate my relationship with my stepdaughter, there are many times when I feel as though I've failed her. I wasn't as loving or patient or communicative as I could have been. I have a long list of my shoulda, coulda, wouldas with her. I can offer the excuse that I'd never done the stepmothering thing before—and that would be true. I can blame her and tell you that she didn't make it easy for me to love her, or sometimes even to like her—and that would be true. There were times when she treated me with contempt, or worse, when she tolerated me or just simply ignored me unless she needed me to do something, say, move out of her way. But honestly, offering excuses wouldn't be good enough. The truth is, I need to take most of the responsibility for our relationship.

She's a kid, and she's working in and through her pain. The times I messed up with her were the times I chose not to follow the Holy Spirit's whisperings. The times I screwed up royally were the times when I allowed my insecurities and pride and pure stupidity to take control, when I chose to act like the child instead of the adult. When I—gasp—acted a lot like the wicked stepmother.

I'm ashamed to say there were many times when I didn't want to do the right thing, when I didn't want to make the effort to reach out. I wanted to feel jealous or immature or superior. Those are not proud moments for me. Those memories are some of the most painful of my life. I just flat out did some things wrong. And I caused some of the heartache in my marriage because of it.

Can you relate?

parent or friend? ally or enemy?

Scott's daughter was fifteen when Scott and I started dating. We dated for six years—that long because we felt that she'd been through so much pain in the divorce, that it wouldn't be fair for her to have to share her father during those delicate teenage years. So we waited until she was in college to marry.

Our relationship was probably like most where adolescent or teenaged children are involved: tensely polite. I did everything I could think of to be hip, to be her friend. I had no interest in being her mother. One mother is usually enough for any child.

But there was something so precious, so special about Scott's daughter. She was a great kid! She had a keen wit and a beautifully sensitive nature. Who doesn't want a child like that? Who doesn't want a friend like that?

I struggled with feeling accepted. And that was the heart of the problem. I desperately wanted to be her friend. When I didn't feel that acceptance, I reacted negatively, out of hurt.

But I learned an important lesson. I can't make someone like me. I can't make my stepchild think of me as a great friend—or a great anything, for that matter.

She had never been a stepdaughter before. She was struggling privately through a divorce. She didn't ask for Mom and Dad to break up, and she didn't ask for her mother to take off when she was just entering adolescence. And she certainly didn't ask for me to join in on her fun-fest called "life."

Really, I don't blame her. I don't blame any kid who has to feel his or her way through divorce.

This chapter is not about becoming the world's greatest step-parent in order for your stepchild to "rise up and call you blessed." There are plenty of good books on the market that will tackle that near impossibility. But children do affect marriage. For better or for worse—and sometimes for worst.

That's what I want to deal with in this chapter.

things to remember

To be fair, young children are a different lot. They're still at that point at which they really don't understand much of what is happening. The children of divorce I'm talking about are adolescent children and older (even adult children!)—the ones more easily swayed by the guilt of the ex. Their minds are active enough to conjure up hatred and mischief. Their tongues become gifted at spewing nasty statements. And let's not forget about those rolling eyes.

But before we get focused on the behavior that comes from their pain, keep a few important things in mind.

These are the lost kids, the innocents. With a divorce, children are the ultimate victims, or losers. Then Mom or Dad finds someone to marry, and guess who gets the shaft again? Yep. Children feel things intensely if they're the ones stuck in the middle between a mom and dad who don't get along. They may act okay, but in the depths of their soul, during the night when they are alone with their thoughts, they feel raw from the wounds that we have caused.

With remarriage, as spouses, we've found our "security," someone else to love and accept us. Kids haven't. They're often left to fend for themselves. *No one truly understands me,* they think.

Special occasions are the worst for them, although the everyday occurrences can create plenty of challenges after divorce and remarriage too. Every birthday, holiday, wedding, or funeral is potentially a nightmare as kids wrestle with traditions (or the lack of them), split attentions and loyalties, and greater disappointments at a time when expectations are especially loaded.

During our first Christmas season together as a married couple, my stepdaughter helped decorate the house and tree. It was the most awkward experience for us! She would pull out ornaments that were from her mother's side of the family and wasn't quite sure what to do with them. I knew what I wanted to do with them: burn 'em! But since that wasn't an option, I watched her place them toward the back and the bottom of the tree. My heart ached as I watched the scene, helpless to change anything.

When a stepparent enters the scene, children see their status in the family knocked down another notch.

One recently remarried friend told author Georgia Shaffer, "My life is more complicated than ever. I've put all this effort into a new marriage, but we're struggling. My new stepson ignores me. His attitude is 'I'm here to be with my dad and that's it.' I feel horrible—like a second-class citizen in my own home."[1]

It's vital that we put ourselves in their shoes and remember, even in the midst of their mischief and heated, obnoxious remarks, that they are reacting out of their reality and working out of their own pain.

When Molly remarried she was afraid that her four children would become estranged from her. They disliked her husband. "I believe subconsciously they thought, *How dare this man invade on our space?*" she says. "I was the center of their lives, and they were the center of mine. Now some man 'took' their place."

marriage under the microscope

Your children and stepchildren are watching everything you and your spouse do. They're watching to see how you solve conflicts, they're watching to see if you're going to stay together. That means it's critical that we put our marriage first. If your marriage is going to succeed, you have to fight for it—not against it. That means that sometimes the children are going to feel as if they're taking the backseat. Notice I say *feel*. Because the reality is that if you put your marriage first, if you put everything into that marriage to make it succeed, you're going to provide those children with a good, balanced, stable home. You'll become role models for them. (Of course, sometimes people who are in love have the tendency to focus on the new boyfriend/girlfriend/spouse so much that they ignore their children or don't treat them or the situation with sensitivity. It's important for parents to beware of this tendency so that children truly don't take the backseat.)

Stepfamily Association of America (SAA; www.saafamilies.org) notes that most blended families will take between four and seven years to fully adjust to the "new" family. That means there's the potential for seven years of stress in your marriage.

The problem often comes when we become surprised by the difficulties in this new blended family. Family therapist Nancy Boyd-Franklin says, "We all enter into a stepfamily with the hope, more like a fantasy, that our situation will be different."[2] Don't be surprised. Expect the unexpected, then plan for it.

stepparent boot camp

As they say, if you can survive blending a family, you can survive anything. So let's look at some things we can do for our marriage to survive this adjustment period with children and spouse intact.

Be the adult. When Eileen found out she was moving into Lee's house, she wasn't exactly thrilled. All that history that was attached to the house, plus Lee's daughter, Annie, had been the "mistress" of the house and Eileen was entering her territory. She knew Annie was having a difficult time with the divorce. So Eileen opted not to make major changes right away. She left decorating the way it was so Annie would still feel comfortable. After about a year, Eileen had a garage sale and got rid of everything that had belonged to Lee's ex-wife—even the kitchen utensils. Lee and Eileen told Annie that she was free to take whatever she wanted, and then everything else went. Annie seemed to be fine with the decision. She even opted to clean her room and sell some stuff.

While Eileen and Lee were sifting through the house, Eileen felt God impress upon her, *Give everything—all the money—to Annie, even give the money you make off your own personal items.* Eileen thought about it and felt at peace with that decision, "which itself is a miracle considering I'm a tightwad to the nth degree," she admits.

The weekend for the sale came. It was so big, Eileen asked her parents to come help.

The first morning of the sale, Lee's ex called and talked to Annie. All Eileen heard was, "Mom, she's getting rid of everything." But Annie still seemed okay. Until the second morning of the sale.

Annie's mom called again, and Annie talked in hushed tones. "When she hung up the phone," says Eileen, "she was a completely different person. She started to make a big deal about getting all her money for the things she sold. She went to every item that was hers and put her name on it, and made sure I kept track of all her items."

That's when Eileen remembered the conversation she'd had earlier with God. Eileen took her mom aside and said, "I don't know why, but I really feel as though I'm supposed to give all this money to Annie." Eileen's mom said, "Well, that's fine to give the money from Lee's stuff. But you should keep the money from your stuff."

"No, because then it would get too complicated. I'm just going to give it all. Honestly, I don't want it."

"I felt such peace about it," says Eileen. "But I was hurt to watch Annie scour over the numbers, eyeing me closely to make sure I didn't cheat her out of anything."

At the end of the weekend, Eileen counted out all the money. She counted Annie's money, which was about one hundred dollars, and gave it to her. Then she made a big deal of counting the rest of the money. Eileen said, "Okay, Lee and I made more than five hundred dollars." Then she placed it in an envelope and handed it to Annie.

"Here," Eileen told her. Annie had a blank look that said, *I'm not comprehending.*

"Annie, your dad and I want you to have this. We're going to put it in a CD for you, so that when you graduate from college, you'll have it, and it will be doubled." Annie started to cry and ran from the room.

"That wasn't anything I would have done on my own," admits Eileen. "I felt God lead me to do that before the whole ex-wife scenario played out. I couldn't have planned that on my own. But God was watching out for our family. Because Lee and I chose to be obedient to his desire, he took care of us. Annie ended up making more than six hundred dollars. I cleaned my house of its tangible history. And Lee's ex-wife got the 'paranoid' award. A winning combination."

My friend Julie told me, "God is assuring me that nothing will be lost at this point if I drop my end of the rope and let the other side appear to win. It is a total paradox. The more I let go, the more peaceful and secure I feel that God is taking care of the situation for me. I no longer have anything to prove."

Establish firm boundaries. Janie found out quickly that she and her husband would need to set boundaries when his children came to visit. When Janie would ask for help setting the table for dinner, her thirteen-year-old stepdaughter, Rhonda, would say, "No, you're not our mom. You can't tell us what to do."

"Come on," she told them. "Help me get dinner ready."

Rhonda said, "Mom said we don't have to listen to you."

"Of course, then I said something stupid like, 'Well, this is my house, and if you want to stay here, you'll do as I say!'" says Janie.

Obviously, that didn't soften the relationship. Finally, Janie took her stepdaughters out to lunch and told them, "This is our house together. You can draw lines for me as your step-mom—things you just want me to stay out of. But I have that right too. Let's talk about our boundaries and then respect each other's. Okay?"

Never bad-mouth the ex to the children. If stepchildren make comparisons between you and the natural parent or share unkind remarks with you, don't take the bait to cast an insult. Keep your feelings to yourself, because it will inevitably get back to your stepchildren. Or it may force your spouse to feel he has to take sides—and guess who will most likely lose? You.

If you can't make positive statements about the ex in front of the children, at least attempt neutral ones.

My friend Carmen once told me, "I never bad-mouthed my children's father. I have permanent bite marks in my tongue because of that." Whatever you have to do.

Encourage play dates. I would always encourage Scott to take his daughter out to dinner or to a movie, to do something as just the two of them. Scott always fought me on this. I'm not sure why. Maybe because he felt we needed to be a "family."

Children need that reassurance that their natural parents still love them and want to spend time with them. Encourage your spouse to do this with his children.

Family meetings are essential. Define the roles of each member of the stepfamily. Don't just wing it. Gina and Andy gathered their children once a month for an ice cream social/family meeting. There they would talk through everyone's chores and expectations. Then they would open the discussion for whatever anyone wanted to say.

"Our only rules were that everyone had to use 'I feel' statements rather than 'you should.' And 'I feel you are a jerk' doesn't work," says Gina. "Then for every complaint, that person would need to come up with a positive response to solve it."

Family meetings keep everyone communicating and on the same page. I wish we would have done this sooner. We just went where the wind blew us, and it made for some difficult times at the Kolbaba residence. I know that's not what any of us wanted, but often we didn't know any better. Instead, Scott and I would have family meetings, which didn't help much because his daughter, who was living with us, didn't know what was going on. How could she invest in the family when she wasn't part of the meetings?

Deal with jealousy. There were several times when I told Scott in the heat of an argument that I felt as though I were the mistress—and his daughter was the queen. So many times, divorced parents will lavish their children with presents and little to no boundaries because they feel guilty over the divorce. It's difficult to watch this and become frustrated and *not* heard.

I found there were times when I struggled with jealousy toward my stepdaughter. This wasn't my prevailing attitude toward her. When she has allowed me into her life, I've been blown away by what a precious person she is. But every once in a while, I would see how Scott could favor her, how he would take her side on an issue and not mine. The pain of those instances would cause me to become jealous. And the jealousy turned into nastiness. I would become snippy, or worse, would ignore her. I'm not proud of those times. I shake my head in shock as I think of them even now. Yet, there they are. Ugly, immature, and definitely not God-honoring.

Avoid the competition trap. "You aren't my real parent, I don't have to listen to you . . ." One bit of advice: just don't go there. Don't take the bait. Remember, it is bait.

Keep a united front. Children will always try to push the boundaries of a second marriage. They will watch to see who is taking the leadership and will play against that. Once they see who is really in charge, they will begin to use one set of parents against the other to achieve their own goals. Make sure you and your spouse stay united in front of them. If you have a disagreement, handle it in private when the children are not around.

Remember who you married. Children tend to suck up our time until our marriage gets squeezed off to the side. You need to set boundaries for your marriage—the good kind of boundaries that state you will not allow a day to go by without hugging and kissing each other, without telling each other at least one thing you appreciate about your spouse, that you will connect with each other about something un-child-related. Zealously guard your date nights and keep the subject of children and exes off limits.

Get rid of the guilt! Often there resides in the biological parent a deep sense of guilt over what has happened to the children.

112

While that's understandable, it can often damage the new marriage. Early in their marriage Dean told Beth, "My children will always come first." "And he was right," Beth says. "He spoiled them. He gave them whatever they wanted. He would take them on trips without me!" Five years into their marriage, their relationship is dangling by a thread.

Parents will tend to overlook boundary issues because of guilt. Do not allow this to happen. Talk to your spouse honestly but candidly. Watch diligently because it can even happen secretly. Beth found out that her husband was buying the kids whatever they wanted, whenever they wanted. This penalizes the present and future marriage relationship for something that happened in the past.

the "ours" equation

There's also the question of you and your spouse having children: the "ours" equation. Scott and I are still dealing with this. I want children. Scott isn't sure if he does or not. He gives plenty of excuses, but I think at least some of the reason he's hesitant is that deep down he fears I'll leave him like his first wife did, and that he'll have to rear our children just as he did his first family.

If you opt to have little darlings that "bind" the blood, then I would recommend you discuss this with your current children. You're not asking their permission; you're communicating with them. You're giving them respect—saying, "You matter to us." And you are helping them understand that you aren't in any way trying to create "our" baby as a replacement or as a way of leaving the current children on the "outside."

stepping in

When I dreamed of becoming a mother, the word never had *step* attached to it. And yet, that's where I find myself. Because the reality is, I love my husband, and he's a package deal. So if I want

113

my marriage to work, I need to pray and tolerate and be patient about those things I can never change: his child. Scott desperately wanted me to like his daughter because she was an extension of him. If I liked and accepted her, in a sense, I liked and accepted Scott. That knowledge has helped me keep from giving up on my relationship with her during some of the difficult times. I've also noticed that when my relationship with her is working okay, my husband seems more relaxed and attentive to me.

for *even* after

Expect kids to test the boundaries of your marriage. They will. Every time. Even adult children! As Macaulay Culkin says in the movie *Uncle Buck*: "I'm a kid, that's my job."

Rather than calling your spouse's children "stepchildren," why not call them "bonus children"? Hearing "bonus child" can do amazing things for a kid—and for his parent. It says, "I'm accepted." For more helpful insight on blended families, check out www.successfulstepfamilies.com.

Don't take it personally, writes Ylonda Gault Caviness in *Essence* magazine. "Recognize that no child is aching to get a stepparent, so from day one assume that you are unwanted and expect a long and sometimes arduous trial period. The child is mournful or angry over the absence of the biological parent and may not necessarily dislike you, she just doesn't like the arrangement."[3]

9

family dealings
{where the hurts never seem to end}

Happiness is having a large, loving, caring, close-knit family in another city.

George Burns

I remember sitting in my new sister-in-law's kitchen, talking with several people about ex-wives. Several members of Scott's family are divorced, so the conversation was enticing.

It became more personal, however, when my sister-in-law made the comment that she missed Scott's ex. "She was always such a risk taker, so much fun. I really miss her."

Mental note: grab ice pick, pull from my gut, grin, and nod politely.

To be fair, Scott's sister is one of my favorite people, and we have a wonderful relationship. And I know she didn't mean to hurt my feelings. She would have been appalled if she'd known how it affected me and how I bled inwardly that night—mostly because I felt she was comparing me to the ex, and I was losing.

Kick insecurity up a notch.

The truth was that she wasn't comparing me. That night I learned an important lesson about families. Just because you and your ex divorce doesn't mean the family moves out of the relationship as quickly as you did.

When Scott's ex-wife left, she created a hole in his extended family. And as much as I'd like for them all to say, "Scott's ex-wife? She was horrible. We never had a relationship with her," the reality is that they did. They share a history with her. They accepted her into their family, and for almost twenty years they loved her as their own. They can't make that disappear any more than I can snap my fingers and have my thighs become twenty pounds lighter. It just ain't gonna happen.

Most families want to accept the "new" spouse. They understand they need to step up to the plate and love the newbie. But this may take some time. While your spouse's family may want to take the risk to accept you into their clan, they may be afraid of being hurt again.

Basically, they have to erase their mental history of the past and start with a fresh motherboard. But the wiring can get tangled and wrapped around the old stuff.

Gina dealt with this with her brother. "My brother had more wives than pennies, it seems," she says. "I knew what a precarious position each new wife was in. She had a tough job coming into a family that had a whole history with some other wife. But every time I connected with a wife—and got to the point I could remember her name and not call her one of the exes'!—my brother would go off and divorce her. It felt almost like a revolving door! Honestly, it made me not want to take the risk anymore. I didn't want to invest the time and energy just to have the relationship snipped off midstream. And it totally wasn't the new wife's fault. It was my brother's!"

Realize it may have nothing to do with you—and everything to do with their risk assessment.

On the other hand, they may feel some resentment because the ex was plucked from their midst. It doesn't matter what you do, sometimes you may feel as though you're on the losing end. They may compare you or say things that set up the ex to be the saint.

One woman I know walked into her mother-in-law's house to find old photos of her husband and his first wife smiling and obviously joyful. "My husband asked his mother to remove the photos. But she just responded with a smile and said, 'I like those photos. I have always loved your first wife.'"

Again, though, it isn't you—it's what you represent. They're still grieving and processing their loss. They've gone through that divorce too, remember. And they may be in the pity party stage or the steaming mad stage.

If this is the case, be careful how you respond. You don't want to give them any fodder for the competition. You'll be the loser. It's out of your control, so acknowledge that it hurts, and feel the pain. You'll be the adult and the winner in the end.

don't jump to conclusions

When my sister-in-law made the comment about how much she missed Scott's ex-wife, I had to make a choice: I could do the pity party thing, which I can be good at, or I could give myself a pep talk. In one of those rare but shining moments of brilliance, I chose the latter.

"Ginger," I told myself, "did she say that to be mean to you?" I knew deep down the answer was no. She had no idea how her words cut me. But I also know she would feel terrible if she knew how she'd inadvertently hurt me. That helped me realize I could let it go.

Do I still remember the statement? Yes. Does it hurt? It could if I let it. Do I harbor anger toward her? No. Every time I think about that experience, I realize God allows me to remember so I can keep in mind the pain divorce causes. I love my sister-in-law, and I don't want her to experience that pain again—not because of me and my husband. I have no control over anybody else's relationship, but I can have some control over mine.

be patient

Once they realize you're here to stay, the risk factor may lessen for them. And eventually they may open up to you. If they never do, what a loss for them! They've missed the opportunity to know a really cool person. (That would be you.)

Janie watched as her sisters-in-law slowly began to open more to her the longer she was married. "They were always polite and pleasant to me," she says. "But they never made me feel as if I really, truly belonged to the family. I was always on the fringe. It was really noticeable when they didn't have a baby shower for me when I was pregnant with my first child." But Janie stuck it out with them and eventually reaped the rewards. "My sisters-in-law began to call me to ask my advice on different topics or to get together to go shopping or do lunch. My patience, while difficult to have at the time, was definitely worth struggling over."

habits are hard to break

Carly had been married to her husband for more than a year when her mother-in-law called her "Marta"—her husband's ex-wife's name.

"It really set me back," Carly admits. "I wanted to yell, 'Do you know I'm different? I'm *not* Marta!'"

More than likely, it doesn't mean anything. It's just a habit. I do that to my dog, for heaven's sake. There are still times when I'll call her by my previous dog's name. Does that mean I hate my new dog? That I resent her for not being my old dog? Not a chance. All it means is that sometimes I experience a brain slip and gain a momentary IQ of 35.

That's it. You could make more of it and overanalyze it to death. But why?

"Come to find out," Carly told me later, "my mother-in-law was horrified by what she'd done. She was so embarrassed. Later, she apologized and tried to console me by telling me it didn't mean anything and that she's glad I'm in her family."

But if Carly's mother-in-law hadn't said anything to clarify, that still doesn't mean she meant what slipped out. She may be too embarrassed to say anything, and afraid that if she does, it will open more of a wound. See it for what it is, a mindless habit, forgive the offense, and move on.

they may be nervous too

If your spouse's family does reach out to you, meet them halfway! Don't make it difficult for them.

I'll always be grateful to my sister-in-law Jeannine. Although she lives in another country, she really went out of her way to connect with me and make me feel special. She didn't have to do that. But she found things that we were both interested in and honed in on those. Now we email each other and review our favorite movies, discuss how her women's Bible study is going, and how my job is.

Sandy had a different experience, though. When her brother married for the third time, she really tried to reach out to her new sister-in-law. "I'd call her to see if she wanted to get together. I tried to find out what she liked to do. But she was pretty closed to me." To the entire family, it turned out. She rarely went to family get-togethers, out to eat, to the movies, anything. "I grew tired of reaching out to her with no response, so I quit," Sandy admits. "I feel badly about it because I know she's struggling with my brother's past relationships. But she's pushed my family away. Now we don't invite her to things because we know she won't come—or if she does, it's on her terms: the time, the place, the length." Sandy and her family, just like many families, will reach out and accept nothing only for so long; then they'll stop reaching out.

I know a lady who is like the sister-in-law in the above scenario. She likes her husband's family but won't get close to them. Then she complains because they've stopped reaching out.

Yes, I refrain from saying, "Duh!" Unfortunately, that relationship won't change for the better until she takes a step toward them.

The steps don't have to be major. You don't have to gush over them or bribe them to like and accept you. Just be sincere. Try to be polite, and act interested in their lives. Find out their likes and dislikes, then drop them a note or email every once in a while "just because."

Little steps, when taken consistently, still get you somewhere. Take those simple steps, and you'll arrive closer to your destination than you may think is possible.

but what if I don't like them?

Every family has some alien who's been plopped down in their midst. We all have them. The dysfunctions ride high.

But before you go out and slash their tires or feed their plants turpentine, consider the words of the apostle Paul in Romans 12:18: "If it is possible, *as far as it depends on you*, live at peace with everyone" (italics added). So put away the tire iron, step away from the creeping ivy, and button your lips when you're really dying to tell Sister-in-law that you think she's an overstuffed prune.

The truth is, you're not in the driver's seat in your spouse's family—especially as a remarried spouse. You're the stranger in their midst. You're the low one on the totem pole, and that means you bear the brunt of the kindness responsibility.

That also means it's best not to admit to your spouse you think your in-laws are kooks. Even if they are, keep that juicy tidbit to yourself. Let your spouse do the bad-mouthing. You can agree silently all you want. But try to keep it silent.

This calls for you to be on your best behavior, to be kind, and "as far as it depends on you" to be a peacemaker.

My friend Lynn watched her mother-in-law, Bonnie, care for Bonnie's first husband's invalid mother for years. "Bonnie's mother-in-law made Bonnie's life miserable while she was married. She felt Bonnie was never good enough." But Bonnie felt God lead her to care for this woman who had treated her so badly. As she did she began to see the woman's demeanor toward her change. And when the woman finally died a year ago, she and Bonnie had forged a close relationship. "My mother-in-law had a draining, difficult time," admits Lynn. "Yet, she did what she felt impressed to do, and I believe God honored her for that. It definitely made Bonnie a gentler person."

I'm not suggesting you run out and volunteer to be caretaker to your spouse's most unlovable family members. But pray about what God *would* have you do.

Sally visits her mother-in-law every Wednesday night. They have dinner together and watch television. "I won't lie and say I love it," says Sally. "Actually, most Wednesdays I dread going. But I made the commitment to live at peace with her. That means I listen quietly when she says things that drive me crazy or that I don't agree with. The funny thing is that since my husband and I have been going to her house, we've seen her soften. She's much more enjoyable to be around."

And on the bright side, when you commit to investing in your spouse's family—even when you don't particularly like them—that makes a huge positive impact on your marriage when your spouse sees you trying to get along with his relatives. He may even "rise up and call you blessed" (Proverbs 31).

A few more things to consider while practicing for sainthood.

hush the bad-mouthing

Delia would often say negative—"but truthful!"—things about her husband's ex to his family. "I couldn't seem to help it! I think

I did it because I figured they were comparing us—and I wanted to come out ahead."

While that sounds nice, there's one problem. Can we say "backdraft potential"? Usually, those statements don't make the ex look bad; they make us look insecure and mean. It is usually best simply to keep quiet—even if the family is involved in a gripe fest about the ex.

Dreadfully, it may get back to the kids (which gives them the upper hand in a power play—or just plain crushes them and doesn't win us any brownie points). You'd be amazed at what little ears can hear . . .

Or it may potentially get back to the ex (which is an "I'm insecure" flare and gives the ex the upper hand in a power play). Eileen was crushed when she inadvertently discovered her sister-in-law was still getting her hair cut from Eileen's husband's ex. "I thought back to all the things I'd said about my husband's ex. I was horrified, and then I was angry. If I hadn't said anything, there would be no news for my sister-in-law to potentially relay. I learned a tough lesson about when to speak and what to say."

discuss where loyalties lie

Scott and I actually met through his sister-in-law, Linda. I have a special place in my heart for her because of that. But several years into our relationship, she and Scott's brother divorced.

When Scott and I became engaged and went over the guest list, I questioned if it would be proper to invite her—after all, she was the reason Scott and I had even met and were together! But Scott's brother was engaged, and after deliberating we decided it was best not to invite her out of loyalty to his brother and out of respect for his fiancée.

Scott and I had to choose where our loyalties would lie. Our loyalties lie first with each other. Second with our family. Third, other people, including the exes.

This doesn't mean, once you choose who's your priority, that life will shake out and be less challenging. Truly, some in-laws are just plain mean. They will say things to hurt. They'll seemingly delight in causing you pain.

Our challenge in these situations is to rise above that, to be more mature, and to consider the source. If they truly are mean, are they really worth getting yourself in a dither over?

Don't waste your energy on them. Instead, focus on loving and enjoying your mate.

for *even* after

If your extended family doesn't accept you, the question then becomes how do you and your spouse accept that family member or members? Several things:

Make sure they don't see how their words or actions affect you. That ups the ante for them.

Treat them with kindness. Margaret Broersma quips: "I've had to cope, long-term, with people who rejected me—people I could never please but for some unavoidable reason were a permanent fixture in my life. After years of trying to guess what would make them happy and often guessing wrong, after acting first one way and then another in response to their inconsistencies, I decided to follow one plan: 'Kill 'em with kindness.'"[1] There's truth in that. King Solomon reminds us, "If your enemy is hungry, give him food to eat; if he is thirsty, give him water to drink. In doing this, you will heap burning coals on his head, and the LORD will reward you" (Proverbs 25:21–22). The apostle Paul adds, "Do not be overcome by evil, but overcome evil with good" (Romans 12:21).

123

Keep your distance. You could always take Jim Smoke's advice. "One should not have to run from family, but when they cause constant conflict in your remarriage, you had better call the movers," he quips.[2] Of course, there's another alternative recommended in the Bible: pray for them and about the situation. Sometimes prayer alone can do the job. Remember the verse that says, "God will go ahead of you. He will fight for you so you don't have to do it" (Exodus 14:14; Deuteronomy 1:30, 3:22).

10

friends

{must they come and go with a spouse?}

You take people as far as they will go, not as far as you
would like them to go.

Jeannette Rankin

"Whoa, whoa, wait a minute," Gina said to her new husband.
"One of your groomsmen and his wife are still close friends with
your ex? The ex who slept around on you? The ex who calls you
all the time and interferes in our marriage? Don't you have a
problem with that?"

"Well, yes," her husband said. "He's one of my best friends. But
I guess I didn't think about the fact that he and his wife would
give all our wedding details to my ex-wife."

It's difficult for friends to take sides. When we divorce we often
subtly place friends in that precarious position of possibly being
forced to choose sides. Sometimes they don't, and both exes are
okay with that. But that seems to be more the exception than
the rule. So friends have two options: stick around and remain
friends, or disappear from sight.

where did they go?

Katie lost her friends in the divorce. "He got custody of the friends," she joked to me. "When I was married to Paul, all our friends were his associates. Obviously, they didn't keep in touch with me."

"Did that bother you?" I asked her.

"Sure," she told me. "They were my friends too. But I understand their reasons for leaving me alone."

Why do friends disappear? There may be several reasons.

They may not agree with the remarriage. They may not have agreed with the reasons for the divorce and remarriage. So in order to take a stand for their convictions, they may decide it's best not to continue a relationship.

Several years ago I discovered that two close friends of mine were involved in an affair. She was married, with three children. It seemed that I was the last to know what had been happening. What was worse—I'd defended them to other friends when the rumors of an affair started.

"No way," I'd said. "Diana's married. There's no way Bob would sleep with her. I don't believe it. Not them."

So imagine my shock and dismay when over a Chinese dinner of kung pao chicken, they blurted the news that they'd been having an affair for three months and they loved each other.

I wasn't sure what to say: "Congratulations"? "I'm honored you told me personally"? "I hope you find all the happiness"?

Actually, I didn't say anything. I just sat there. And sat there. All I could think was, *I defended you!*

Finally, Bob shifted uncomfortably in his seat, and Diana's smile faded. "Look," Bob said, "we know what you're going to say."

Now I was intrigued—especially since *I* didn't know what I was going to say. He continued, "Diana's divorcing Don, and we're getting married."

Still I didn't say anything. My silence forced them to defend their actions—even though I'd made no judgments on them or had given no indication I would. They continued to spill the secret. Diana's marriage had been in trouble, and so she'd gone to Bob for comfort.

I finally told them, "Look, you're my friends, and I care deeply about both of you. However, you need to know I don't agree with the choices you've made. Those choices, while they may feel right to you, carry heavy consequences that will last forever. I just can't be happy for you when I know what you're doing is wrong."

I guess I should have felt honored that they still asked me to sing at their wedding.

So Bob and Diana married (sans me as the vocalist) and left a hurricane-sized mess in their wake. But at least they're happy. That's what counts, right?

As I discussed the situation with Scott, I finally realized that I needed to make a break with them—not out of hatred or judgment or moral superiority, but simply for my own convictions. After really praying and thinking about it, I felt that I couldn't be true to my convictions and at the same time condone their relationship.

Every once in a while I run into them, and they tell me how they're doing. It isn't awkward; I want the best for them. And I pray that one day they will discover God's mercy and forgiveness.

But the saddest thing is that I miss them. I miss their friendship—not the tainted friendship I would have now. The old friendship—that had an innocence and truth to it. That part is gone.

They may feel disloyal to the ex-spouse. Especially if the friends were closer to the ex or if they were work associates, former classmates, or old roommates.

"When my wife and I were married, we invited my good friends Steve and Jan," says Mike. "They didn't come. No note, no explanation, nothing. I couldn't figure it out because Steve and I had been great friends. Then one day it hit me. Jan and my ex-wife were friends before Steve and I became friends. Because Jan continued her relationship with my ex, Steve felt he needed to be loyal to Jan, who was loyal to my ex. I miss Steve's friendship, but I understand that sometimes people need to move on."

They're processing and grieving the loss. They may still be hurting from their own loss. Remember that the divorce didn't just affect you and your family. Divorce has a ripple effect—it affects friends too.

They may be deeply affected and grieving. They may be processing what happened and trying to figure out their new role. It's as though the game has changed for them. They were going along, playing Candyland, and you switched it to Scrabble.

"I was surprised when so many of my friends left me," says Allie. "That really hurt."

Then one day she ran into a friend. "My friend let it slip that she is still swirling from the divorce. I had no idea that my marriage could affect my friends in such a way."

Many times our friends feel uncomfortable that they're in essence being asked to pronounce where their loyalties lie. They feel forced into the role of diplomatic peacemaker—but it's a no-win situation for them. *Hmmm, which one of my friends am I willing to hurt more?*

They may be confused. They may not know what to do, so it becomes easier not to do anything—to abandon and move on. That doesn't mean they are harsh, mean, or unaffected by the loss.

Then as time goes by, they may feel guilty because they have stopped calling and connecting. So it becomes easier to avoid you, because it would be awkward for them to see you. They no longer feel free to reminisce or joke about the past for fear of offending the new spouse.

So what do you do? If you're not sure why your friends have gone MIA, try to reconnect with them. Send them an email and say, "Hey! I miss our friendship. Is there some way we can reconnect?"

If they respond, great. They may feel free to open up in an email and tell you what's really going on. Or they may respond with a surface reply about nothing being wrong—then you never hear from them again. Take it at face value and move on.

friends to the end

When friends abandon you, they made the decision, and it was out of your control. However, if your friends choose not to leave the relationship, you have some choices to make.

Discuss the relationship with your spouse. Friendships are joint ventures. Make sure you decide together your course of action.

Scott had a couple of close friends that he had shared with his ex-wife. Those friends continue to be good friends with the ex. So Scott and I have had numerous conversations about this.

Many spouses are okay with the "share." Frankly, I struggle with it. Mostly because we've had a lot of boundary problems with his ex-wife. I told Scott that I wasn't comfortable pursuing a relationship with them, mostly because I wasn't sure I could trust them.

"It's as though I feel betrayed before I even enter the relationship," I told him. "I feel as though the friendship has been tainted before it even begins."

As we talked, I discovered he shared the same feelings. That conversation was easy for me to have; I never had the relationship with them, so I had nothing to lose. On the other hand, Scott had everything to lose. He lost his marriage, his in-laws, security, and a complete, whole family. And he also lost his friends.

It was interesting when one evening after church several years later, we bumped into them at a restaurant. We joined them and tried to catch each other up on our lives. There was only one problem: I had nothing to catch up on. They discussed people, places, and situations that had happened "pre-Ginger." I was intensely uncomfortable as I felt promptly forgotten and overlooked. No one even bothered to fill me in on the history or who the people were they were discussing.

Do you remember when you were a kid and you sat at a table surrounded by adults having adult conversation? Yeah, well, that was how I felt the entire night. If only I had my pacifier and security blanket . . .

I just prayed for the evening to be over as soon as possible.

Scott and I had another discussion about the meeting on our drive home.

"I miss them," Scott told me. "But I just can't continue to have a relationship when I know they tried to straddle the fence during the breakdown of my marriage. I just don't know if I can trust them like I used to."

Go with your gut, not your insecurities. This is a topic you definitely need to discuss with your mate. If you're uncomfortable hanging out with the "old" friends, be honest and tell your spouse. If he doesn't understand, then consider a compromise: you could suggest that only he spend time with them. The important thing is to protect your marital boundaries.

If you're uncomfortable with that, you don't have to apologize. Just say it straight, tell your spouse the reason, then let it go.

Set the boundaries. If you choose to remain active friends with the "shared" friends, determine the boundaries of that relationship. Decide what and how much you will share about your marriage. You may even want to limit how often you get together with them.

It seems as though every time Scott and I get together with a couple friends of ours, Daman starts to bad-mouth his ex. During those times I wonder, *When are we going to move on? Will there be a time when we can go through a visit without bringing up the ogre?* I understand that it may be insecurity, but more likely, it's anger and pain surfacing. So when he starts to bring up his ex, I try to subtly change the subject.

Commit to each other that pumping your friends for information about "the other side" is strictly off limits. Ignorance is bliss, they say. In these cases, it's true.

Even if you can trust those friends to keep confidences, why worry about an "oopsie" moment in which something slips? It's best to keep quiet about anything you don't want the ex to "accidentally" or "accidentally on purpose" find out.

find new "innocent" friends

There's something to be said for new friends. They help you move beyond the past. They don't share all the history. They know you and your spouse as you and your spouse, not your spouse and the new wife or husband. There is an easier acceptance without comparisons or judgments. If your new friends don't like you, you know it's you and not because they liked the ex better!

what to look for

Steer clear of couples who are struggling in their marriage. While that sounds harsh, the reality is they will drag you down. It's like the business principle that rich people hold to: if you want to be rich, hang out with people who challenge you, who are richer and smarter and more business-savvy than you. You'll never become rich hanging out with people who have a middle-class mind-set.

The same holds true for your marriage. Diligently seek couples who are working and succeeding at their marriage. That doesn't mean you abandon couples who are struggling. Just don't make them your main confidants. They're already cynical. You are who you hang with. If you hang with people who are distrusting and miserable in their marriage, you may be surprised to awaken one day to the fact that you're complaining more about your spouse and you're more negative toward him or her.

Really, this is a no-brainer, but it's amazing how many people hang around with others who are miserable in their marriages. Don't take advice from people who have been unsuccessful in their situations.

Find friends who will keep you accountable. You want friends who are okay in their marriage, have been married long enough to have been through some challenges and survived with their relationship intact. You want friends who believe in your marriage—not necessarily in the two of you individually. These friends will be a godsend to your marriage if you ever run into a snag. They won't take sides except the one where the marriage takes precedence. Some of the best friends to hold you accountable are those couples who are spiritually active and focused on their faith. You don't want someone who makes you feel spiritually inferior, of course, but someone who can challenge you to think bigger than your own problems.

Regardless of which friends you choose, stay connected with your spouse. If, at any point, either of you has second thoughts about a particular relationship, step back from it, talk about it, pray over it, and then make a decision. Relationships are slow to grow and mature.

for *even* after

Look for friends in all the right places:

- Join a community volleyball or softball league.

- Get involved in a church with an active couples' group for either Bible study or networking.

- Think about folks in your workplace.

- Try the library. Believe it or not, libraries are a great source for connecting with other people. They have book discussion groups, and many of them have movie or music discussion groups as well.

- Become involved in a community theater production.

- Volunteer at a local community center or for a short-term missions trip.

part 3

your marriage

you and your spouse

Fear plays a strong role in second marriages. And it's hard
not to use your fears to manipulate your partner to do
what you want. Say a wife feels panicky every time her
husband is ten minutes late coming home because her
first husband had an affair. It would be wrong to force
her new spouse to adhere to a rigid time schedule, where
his freedom is curtailed. At the same time, it's okay to
admit that some days we're just needier than others. This
wife can occasionally say, "I know it's irrational, but I'm
having a panicky day. Pray for me, and please try to come
home on time today."

GARY OLIVER IN *MARRIAGE PARTNERSHIP* MAGAZINE[1]

11

avoiding the communication crisis

{talk about what ruins—or saves—a marriage}

Pick your battles. Not every hill is a hill to die on.

Unknown

My husband's favorite verse is Proverbs 25:24: "Better to live on a corner of the roof than share a house with a quarrelsome wife." He usually quotes that right before I send him to sleep in the garage.

How is it that the one topic we've had drilled into our heads over and over and over is still one of the most difficult topics for us to master? We know we should communicate. We know how important it is to our marriage. But we're not exactly sure how to put into words—and not just any words, but the right words—what we're feeling and thinking. Half the time, *we're* not even sure what we're feeling. Yet a commitment to practicing the fine art of communication is essential if we want to stay married contentedly.

On the drive home from a recent vacation, my husband and I had an argument in which we fell into our typical pattern of shutdown. Have you ever done this? The conversation isn't going anywhere, you don't feel heard, so you withdraw and stop communicating.

Only this time, I didn't want it to be that way. I didn't want our final day of vacation to be a bust because of bad communication. So I told him, "That's it. This time we're not withdrawing or shutting down the dialogue." So we proceeded to lay into each other, and what did we do? We withdrew. Yep, even after that noble sermon on keeping the dialogue going.

But God got into my brain during that withdrawal period. And for all my excuses of "Yes, but *Scott* . . ." God prompted a truth about *me*: I needed to reconcile. In marriage it really doesn't matter who is at fault in an argument; it's our responsibility to reconcile.

I remember interviewing Stormie Omartian, best-selling author of *The Power of a Praying Wife*, on the topic of prayer and reconciliation. When she mentioned that we need to be the first to make the relationship right, I said, "But it doesn't seem fair that I have to reconcile or make peace when I'm not the one at fault."

She smiled and said, "You're right. I dealt with that issue in my marriage too. But God can work in a relationship only through the person who is willing to be flexible. He asks us to be flexible."

So on our drive back from the Badlands, after I wrestled with my pride for a while, I reached over and laid my hand on Scott's. "Thank you for sharing your thoughts with me. I appreciate it—even though it's difficult to hear. I want you to know that I heard you."

I could feel the tension release from Scott's body, and we were able to talk calmly and reasonably.

Will that same topic come up again? Probably. After all, we're human. We have character issues that won't simply vanish, so we're stuck wrestling with them, while being open to listen and willing to keep trying.

name it and claim it

Half the battle in communication is figuring out what we're feeling. How are we supposed to share accurately our feelings, to "communicate," when we have no idea what it is we really want or need to say?

Janie admitted that she doesn't always stop to think what she's feeling. "Usually, I spout off, then think about what I should have said!"

If your spouse has done or said something that bothers you, before you confront him or her, ask yourself some questions:

- Could my mate's fear, stress, worry, or hurt have provoked her action or words?
- Is he reacting more to his own painful past than to me?
- Did my spouse say or do that to hurt me on purpose?
- What am I feeling? Am I angry? Frustrated? Hurt?
- Am I feeling insecure? Why?
- Does this stem back to my previous marriage?
- Am I misreading or exaggerating his actions?

Answer honestly, so you can tell your mate, "I felt frustrated when you came home late tonight and didn't call me. It brought back the paranoia from when my ex-husband would stay out late and I discovered he was having an affair. And that scared me."

When we can name exactly what we're feeling, it allows us to confront gently and with more clarity. It also usually keeps our spouse in the dialogue.

137

those darn expectations

It's impossible to enter marriage without certain expectations. We expect our spouse to love and respect us, to remain faithful and loyal to us, to be our companion and encourager.

However, some expectations are unrealistic and unfair. Author Jim Smoke writes, "It is easy to compile a long list of what did not happen in a prior marriage and expect your new list to be fulfilled in the first three months. Hope often lies in your new spouse doing all the things that your former spouse did not do: namely, fulfill all of your new expectations."[1]

It's important that we consciously reprogram our expectations, and define and understand our new spouse. It's important to tell ourselves, "She is not my ex, and I can't expect her to fulfill what my ex never did." Or, "I can't expect him to respond the same way my ex did; the way I'm used to." If our first spouse became loud and confrontational when angry, we can't expect that our current spouse will. This one may become quiet and withdrawn.

the do's and don'ts of communicating

So how do you navigate those murky waters of communication?

1. Do be honest. Hiding your feelings from your spouse does nothing but frustrate you and eventually perplex your spouse. "Keep absolutely no secrets from each other," says Molly. "My current husband and I pledged that we would discuss every-thing—even the difficult things. And we would agree to disagree. But at least everything would be out in the open."

2. Do bring up an issue with your spouse within twenty-four hours, or forget about it. Carly says, "It seems as though there are communication issues that you assume are going to get handled. It's important not to allow these things to remain hanging over."

3. Do keep to the issue. If you start a discussion about who should babysit your daughter and end up arguing over discipline issues, you've moved off track. Take a break and return to the issue when you both are sane, rational, and calm.

4. Don't withdraw! If you're not happy with the way the discussion is turning out, you may be tempted to withdraw because of self-preservation or as a punishment to your spouse. But to some people, withdrawal feels like abandonment. If you need to take a time-out, tell your spouse you need some time to think and clear your mind before you continue the discussion.

5. Watch what you say. You may think it will feel good to say something you've been dying to say and that you feel you have every right to say. But be careful. Those are always the times when I find those words don't give me the pleasure I thought they would.

Last year, Scott and I decided to trailer our motorcycle out to Yellowstone. We live in Chicago, a metropolitan area in which we should have been able to find a trailer to rent. Instead, the weekend before we were to leave on vacation, Scott went on eBay and purchased one—in Richmond, Virginia. We had to drive a forty-eight-hour round trip to pick up a trailer that would have been cheaper to rent or purchase in our area.

Granted, the trip was an adventure, and we did have a lot of fun going. But the trailer probably wasn't the wisest eBay purchase. No big deal. At least, it wasn't until I made it one in the middle of an argument several weeks later. Because I felt as though I was "losing" the argument, I brought up his purchasing decisions and how irresponsible he had been.

Technically, was I right? Yes, and he knew it. But did it strengthen our relationship? Nope. It hurt it—and it dampened the fun memories of that trip. Was it worth it? Nope.

So I was "right." So what. What did I really win from being right? How did my marriage win from my being correct?

The apostle Paul tells us, "Do not let any unwholesome talk come out of your mouths, but only what is helpful for building others up according to their needs, that it may benefit those who listen. And do not grieve the Holy Spirit of God, with whom you were sealed for the day of redemption" (Ephesians 4:29–30).

That's a goal I've been working toward. If the words won't edify, I'm learning to keep my big mouth shut.

If that's not enough incentive, here's what Jesus had to say: "I tell you that men will have to give account on the day of judgment for every careless word they have spoken. For by your words you will be acquitted, and by your words you will be condemned" (Matthew 12:36–37).

Before you say anything, think about the consequences. If you still have trouble holding your tongue, before you say anything you will regret, ask if you can talk at another time. That will give you a chance to calm down, think rationally, and consider your response without the heat of the immediate situation.

6. Don't criticize. You can complain—offer something specific and limited to the situation. But criticism can involve blame and character attacks. And criticism is sure to put your spouse on the defensive.

7. Don't make threats. "If you . . . then I'll . . ." "You'd better not . . ." "Don't you ever say or do that again, or I'll . . ." First, this puts your partner on the defensive. And someone on the defensive will never be able to hear you—which means no change will happen. It doesn't motivate anybody. It doesn't solve anything or resolve anything.

8. Do take a break if the discussion becomes too intense. Sometimes in a heated argument, one spouse may shut down and stop reacting. This is usually called stonewalling, and it's a protective mechanism. To the other spouse, though, it can signal disapproval, smugness, or superiority. So take a time out when the topic gets too heated. Calm down, take some deep breaths, and soothe yourself.

9. Don't play the blame game. This makes up a majority of the letters I receive in my office. And when I ask counselors about the most common pattern of behavior and communication, a majority of them announce, "People love to blame their partners for the trouble in their relationship." Of course, it's never our fault. So it must be our spouse's.

Really listen to your spouse's complaints, think them over before you discard them as ludicrous. They may have a tiny kernel of truth in them. If so, be the mature person that you are and accept responsibility.

When Beth and Dean would argue, he would become verbally abusive toward her. When she would confront him about his attitude and actions, he would respond, "That's just the way I am. I can't help it."

That is not truth. We use that excuse because we're too lazy or afraid to take responsibility for ourselves. We can choose our responses. We can choose how to react.

Psychologist Kent Hughes says this about blame: "The most frequent statement I hear is, 'You make me so mad!' I don't dispute that often we feel angry in response to another's action. But it's inaccurate to say that someone makes us feel angry. Your emotions are in your control."

Carly learned early in her marriage not to throw things in her husband's face. "I learned my husband stays in the discussion and doesn't become defensive if first I talk about how much I love him, how much I want our marriage to work, and what I love about him. Then I gently bring up the situation: 'I've noticed that in these situations, you act this way. I'm wondering if it's a reflection of something that's unresolved from your previous marriage. If it is, would you consider talking to a professional who can help you work through that issue so it no longer affects our relationship? That simple step would make me respect your decision to work on this relationship.'"

10. Do say no to the "D" word: _divorce_. You've probably heard this one from just about every marriage counselor, pastor, teacher, "expert." _Yeah, yeah,_ you think. _I know._ But it's amazing how easily this little word can pop into our head, and worse, our mouth. This isn't just about not using the word; it's about not even thinking the word. Be proactive. That includes "fake outs," such as, "Well, then, why did we even get married?"

"You may think you have an understanding about divorce," says Carly. "But it's still good to verbalize that it's not a choice in your marriage. When my husband and I went through a difficult financial time, I kept thinking, *It's not an option. We're always going to be together.* I could feel confident about that because we verbalized that understanding."

11. **Don't make assumptions about your spouse.** Truthfully, I don't know what's going on in my spouse's head. Until I ask him. Rather than assuming something that may be purely a figment of your imagination, ask. "I was surprised when you said that. I felt that was insensitive. What was going on in your mind? Did you mean that? Or am I reading something into your words that isn't there?"

12. **Don't assume your spouse can read your mind.** If I don't tell my spouse my expectations, he doesn't know them. Period. Carly told her husband, "These are things I dealt with in my first marriage, and we have to set rules—especially over who will do what chore. We have to take care of these expectations so we know what's going on with each other."

13. **Don't be quick to discourage.** If your spouse wants to do or try something, be careful not to say no too quickly. Try, "Let me think about that." Then really think about it! Maybe it's not something you want to do, but your spouse really does. Could you be willing to try it? It may open more lines of communication rather than shutting them off right away.

14. **Timing is everything.** Talking about visitation schedules in front of the children probably isn't the best idea if you know it could lead into an argument. Find a private time, when both of you are wide awake. (Hint: bedtime and when you're hungry are not good times to bring up a topic of discussion.)

15. **Leave the bodies buried.** Do not keep digging up your old spouse. Don't think that the problems you had before are destined to repeat themselves.

"That's one of the things I did right," says Carmen. "I didn't focus on what went wrong in my previous marriage, thinking that those would be the same problems. I tried to make changes in myself. I tried to curb my tongue."

Avoid at all costs "You're just like her" and "My ex would have done it this way." Of course, the comparison may not even be a bad or negative thing. For instance, if you're watching an old movie, and you say, "The first time I saw that movie was at a drive-in. Of course, I never really *saw* the movie. I was with John and we, you know . . . it was a *drive-in*." How rude is that? You're not being mean or rubbing it in your current beloved's face. It happened, it's a memory. There are good parts of every marriage. As time mellows you, you do remember those good parts. But you don't have to talk about them!

Whenever someone says "What you just did reminds me of my former spouse" is like throwing a bomb into the situation. (It's kind of like telling your spouse, "You're just like your mother"—it's usually not meant as a compliment.) Those words can be so destructive and demeaning. Let's face it, who wants to be compared to a failed spouse?

be honest about the trust issue

Part of communication involves trust. Janie remembers that the first year she and Sam were married, Sam's ex-wife kept showing up to cause trouble. One day Janie arrived home from work to discover her husband talking with his ex-wife, who had pulled into their driveway, had him cornered, and was talking nonstop. So Janie quietly moved into position where she could hear everything they were saying without being discovered.

"I'm not proud to say I reduced myself to sneaking around and eavesdropping on my husband," admits Janie. "But I wanted to hear what his ex had to say. Not only that, I wanted to hear how Sam was relating to her when I wasn't around." In other words, Janie didn't trust Sam; she didn't yet trust their relationship.

Later that evening, she confronted him. "I prayed before I did it," she says. "Then I waited for a calm moment and told him what I'd heard." At first, Sam was upset. But she explained that she was feeling insecure because she didn't feel he respected her enough to draw boundaries with his ex-wife.

"I figured it was better to tell him the truth than to keep quiet and let it eat me up," says Janie. "He was hurt that I still didn't trust him completely. But once he understood, he said he would try to show me that he did respect me and our marriage."

ghosts of conflicts past

While Scott and I were dating, I overheard a country song on the radio one day that really struck me. Tricia Yearwood was singing "The Woman Before Me and You."

The chorus went, "The woman before me must have been hard on you cause that look in your eyes I never put you through. Sometimes I think you must be talking to the woman before me and you."

One of the consequences of being the "next" spouse is that we're stuck holding the baggage of the previous "owner." If his ex used tears as a manipulative strategy, don't hold your breath for sympathy when you start to cry in front of him. Your tears, however sincere and innocent, will act as a mental trigger, and will push a button within his head that says, *Danger! Danger! Manipulation coming on.*

Jennifer remembers the first time her second husband didn't come home when he said he was going to and he didn't call. That was a big issue of resentment and distrust in her first marriage. But when she explained to him why that pushed a button for her, he never did it again.

"Through the five years we have been together," says Jennifer, "when I have overreacted to something he does, he has assured me, 'I am not your ex.' Through his patient 'proving of himself,' which isn't really fair, he has earned my trust. Now I don't react to things like I used to."

Sometimes remarried spouses become hyper-vigilant about even little things. Things that would normally not be a big deal all of a sudden become misinterpreted and blown out of proportion. It can become easy to assume the worst.

While it's unfair, it may become your responsibility to "prove" yourself. But the more you do, the more your spouse will be able to trust and see that you are not, in fact, the ex.

the importance of healing words

I met with a writer at a conference a year ago who made an interesting statement about her marriage: "I would not be the person I am today if my husband hadn't used words to heal and comfort me." This woman had been sexually abused as a child and felt unlovable and unlovely. But her husband would tell her, "You are the most beautiful woman I know."

"At first I wouldn't believe him," she admitted to me. "I would tell him to be quiet and stop telling me things that he didn't mean."

It took a lot of prayer and time, but his words started to sink in to her soul, and she began to realize that it was her feelings, and not his words, that were incorrect. "God started to work on me through my husband's words; then I began to realize, I am beautiful! I am lovable."

When Scott and I were first dating, he'd tell me I was meek. *Excuse me—meek?* I thought. *What a terrible thing to say!*

But he told me, "I see that wall you have around yourself. I can also see that behind the wall is a beautiful, meek, sensitive woman."

He saw something in me that I didn't want to see in myself. His words made me want him to see my meek, sensitive side.

On my end, I often tell Scott, "I'm not going anywhere. You're stuck with me!" We joke about it, but the underlying current is a comfort. I'm telling him that no matter what happens, we are doing life together until we die.

A few things to keep in mind about healing words:

- **Use them often.** If you think your spouse is beautiful, funny, smart, a good money manager, a nice dresser, a charming person, tell her. Your spouse will never know unless your thoughts make it to your mouth. Your words help to build trust.
- **Make them sincere.** During Cheri's first marriage, her husband would say "I love you" in the same way he'd say, "This was a good day." It didn't have the meaning behind it.
- **Think of your words, especially "I love you," as holy**, particularly the second time around. After all, your spouse heard those words the first time, and look what happened.
- **Tell the "why."** Often when Eileen would tell Lee "I love you," he'd come back with "Why?" He would call her on it and want to know the reasons behind her words. The reasons were important to Lee because during his first marriage, his wife would reluctantly tell him she loved him, only after he would say it first. In the meantime, she was more interested in other men, so her words were empty.

  "When Rick says 'I love you,'" says Carly, "I'll ask, 'What made you say that at this moment?' He usually identifies it. He'll say, 'I was just looking at you sitting there and thinking about how much I love you.' And I'm sitting in an old stained T-shirt, I haven't washed my hair or brushed my teeth. I'm thinking, *Yeah, right.* But for some reason, it works. It means more when he identifies it."

  Start saying "I love you"—then make it count. Tell your spouse, "I love you because . . ." "I love this about you. I love that about you."
- **If you receive healing words, it is okay to ask the "why."** Otherwise, you may go through your marriage thinking, *He just loves me because I cook him dinner* or *She just loves me because of sex.* And that may not be it at all. Asking the question is important. Don't assume too much.

146

- **If you receive healing words, accept them.** For years into their marriage, Katie was suspicious of the words "I love you." "My first husband would say them, but it always felt as though he were trying to convince himself," says Katie. "My current husband says it all the time. One day I told him, 'Please don't say "I love you" so much, because it gets cheap.' He said, 'But I mean it.' I told him, 'Yes, but if you say it too much I feel you're just saying it to have something to say. Make sure you say it at the right time—not when you're watching football or whatever.'" Later, though, she realized, *Who am I to tell him when to say he loves me?* "I'm sure that conversation stemmed directly from my first marriage," she admits. So now her husband doesn't say the words "I love you" as much anymore. But that doesn't mean he hasn't gotten creative! Now he says other things: "I miss you," "I'm no good without you." It's still saying "I love you," but in a different way. "I'm learning to accept what my husband says," says Katie. "And you know what? I like what he says. He makes me feel better about myself and our marriage."

problem solvers ltd.

Here's a news flash: it doesn't matter how much talking and begging and arguing and cajoling you and your spouse do, there will be some problems or issues that will never change. For the more than ten years Scott and I have been together, we've fought over the same topics over and over and over. And I have this sneaking suspicion that in thirty years, we'll still be arguing over the same things. In some ways we're incompatible. But if I've learned one thing from my marriage and my role at *Marriage Partnership* magazine, it's that nobody is compatible.

Renowned family psychologist John Gottman says: "It's a myth that if you solve your problems, you'll automatically be happy. Couples need to know that they may never solve most of their problems."[2] That's the point of marriage, I think. God designed men and women to be different in order to complete and complement each other—and that's a lifetime job for us to get it right. Together we make a whole entity. That means Scott brings things to the relationship that I need in my life. But God put Scott there with those characteristics and desires in order to teach me more about the way God in the Triune works.

Our job is to learn how to live out those incompatibilities. Yes, that includes offering and receiving grace. But the more we commit to accepting and understanding our incompatibilities, the more our family and neighbors and friends and church and work communities see God working.

So the next time you have a discussion about something that's driving you crazy, stop for a moment and ask yourself, *What can I learn from this? How can I apply this to my life to make me a better person?* It's okay to continue to push for improvement, but acknowledge your mate's limitations and still communicate some acceptance.

for *even* after

Talk about the ways you like to give and receive love. Pick up a copy of Gary Chapman's book The Five Love Languages.

Tell each other when you're struggling or when you're having a rough day.

Talk, and keep talking about it. Try not to close the door of communication. If you're feeling insecure, tell your spouse. It's okay.

Keep short accounts—don't bottle up your fears or anger or doubts until they explode.

12

sex

{it ain't what it used to be}

> Sex becomes the laboratory where you're really going to
> find out about unfinished business. You're going to no-
> tice if somebody's reluctant. Don't overlook those things.
>
> Robert Roop, Christian sex therapist

Sally and Matthew had their first argument on their honeymoon, and it was about sex. "I had this assumption that all men were sex maniacs," she says. "I was ready to go. And he wasn't ready to give that part of him. I finally asked him, 'What is your problem?' I admit I didn't ask with much tact or sensitivity. Our sex life went downhill from there."

Matthew was still struggling with his ex-wife's betrayal.

"It was very difficult when people would joke, 'Oh, those honeymooners, having sex all the time,'" Sally says. "I could never say the truth. Which was, 'No, actually, we're not. Thanks to his ex-wife.' There was no one to talk to about it."

Sex is different after a divorce. Because sex is the most intimate thing you can share with a spouse, sex can take the hardest hit in a new marriage. Trust, betrayal, anger, hurt—all are things that affect intimacy. Thus, this is one area that needs the most attention in a remarriage.

Because of betrayal issues in Gina's husband's first marriage, intimacy was a rough go for her remarriage. They had to work through a lot of trust issues, and many times she had to be the initiator and encourager. Those times led to frustration and hurt. "We'd have sex, but it felt as though he was holding back," says Gina. When she'd bring it up to Andy, he'd admit she was right, but he would say, "It's not you."

"It's difficult to believe that," says Gina, "when I'm the person with whom he's being intimate."

Finally, they decided to seek some professional help to deal with his sexual baggage from the first marriage.

"I discovered it really isn't about me," says Gina. "It's his ex-wife's unfaithfulness that knocked out a hole in his spirit, and it was going to take some time to heal."

In a recent national *Marriage Partnership* survey, we asked respondents, "In your remarriage, which of the following have posed challenges in the sexual relationship between you and your current spouse?" Thirty-eight percent said "difficulty trusting" and 20 percent answered "fear of rejection."[1]

Sex the second time around encounters a handicap before we even get started.

According to Christian sex therapist Robert Roop, for some people, especially for men, sex becomes the priority in a remarriage. They desire to get back to having a sexual relationship because they were used to that. So they may place pressure on the wife. "They move too quickly into the marital intimacies because they want to move back into the comfort zone," Robert says. "So they marry and never really take the time to bond in other ways. Add to that the pressure of the husband not having a good experience with his first marriage. He thinks, *I want to make sure we have a good sex life because I've been disappointed in the past.* That's why second marriages can be disastrous."

Also, women may enter into a second relationship with certain anxieties that men may not necessarily have. If she's had children, for instance, she's going to have more of a body image issue than she did in her first marriage.

If your sex life is super, feel free to read this chapter to see what others are experiencing. If your sex life isn't what you thought it would be the second time around, however, here are a few things to consider.

unrealistic expectations: when kids are in the picture

The first time you were married, you didn't have children—the passion was free to flow whenever, however, and wherever.

Usually, though, once a couple gets to the point of divorce, the sex is no longer really great, if it's there at all. So we may enter remarriage believing that our spouse is going to fulfill all our sexual desires.

Surprise. It doesn't happen.

I was discussing sex in remarriage with Shay Roop, who is a licensed registered nurse and mental health counselor, board certified in human sexuality by the American Board of Sexology. She told how one of her clients complained that sex with her first husband was better than with her second. Dr. Roop asked her, "Did you go into that first marriage with children?"

"Well, no," the woman answered.

"So, you could have sex in any room, any time of the day or night. You never worried about anybody listening, did you?"

"No."

"Well, gee, things are kind of different now, right?" Shay told her. "You have to wait for a special time. You may be ready to go at 2:00 in the afternoon, but if Johnny has some friends over, you and Hubby are probably not going to retire to the bedroom."

See how a little perspective can make a difference?

Take a look at your own expectations versus realities. If you're struggling with a disappointing sex life, think about these possibilities:

- I didn't have children when I entered my first marriage. I do now.
- In my first marriage, I didn't have to worry about little ears and eyes like I do now.
- My wife didn't enter her first marriage with stretch marks from childbirth.
- My husband didn't enter his first marriage with a pot belly and other signs and wonders of the aging process.

there's hope

If you and your spouse are struggling with intimacy issues, above all else, seek some professional counseling, especially if your first marriage was rife with infidelities. If you don't take care of the past baggage or unrealistic expectations, that becomes tremendously unfair to your current spouse. He or she deserves the best you have to give.

Here are some other things to keep in mind.

1. Determine to laugh a lot. Don't take yourself so seriously in the bedroom. Encourage each other: "We'll get better with time." Then you have diffused what may happen.

2. Guard your sex life. When Scott's daughter was living in our home, her bedroom was right next to ours. So those three years she lived with us—the first three years of our marriage—were lean in the sex department. While that made her life much better—escaping the possibility of having to listen to her father and her stepmother—it could have wrecked our relationship. We had to become creative and make finding time for sex a priority. If she went out with her friends or to visit her mother, bingo!

152

Early in the morning—and quietly!—while she was still asleep. Quickies. Seize the opportunity!

3. Guard your sex thought life. Many remarried spouses live with an unspoken insecurity about their previous relationship. In essence, we allow the ex to come to bed with us. After all, says Dr. Harry Jackson, "Former couples were attracted to each other enough to marry. Many fear that the adage, 'Absence makes the heart grow fonder,' just might come true. Some new spouses may wonder if there's lingering sexual attraction for the ex-husband or ex-wife."[2]

The reality is that you're probably thinking more about your spouse's ex than he or she is! Don't allow the ex to ruin what belongs to you and your marriage. The goal is to erase the old mental tapes from your previous marriage and re-record new ones with your spouse.

One good way is to do a reality check. "I'm not Jill, I'm Brooke. I'm not your first wife." Sometimes that helps you both realize that that was then, this is now.

4. Talk about sex! Sex, in itself, is a form of communication. Therefore, it's a topic that we need to talk about with each other. This is a wonderful step to having a great sex life with your spouse. If you have never had this discussion, it's not too late to start.

Talk about what you like and dislike in sex. Talk about your erogenous zones. Talk about the things that were turnoffs in your former marriage. (Caveat: don't talk about the things your former spouse did that you liked. Your current spouse doesn't need the pressure or to fill his or her mind with thoughts of comparisons.)

Explain, "This is a major turnoff to me. If you did this, I would want to spend the rest of the night in the bathroom. I'd feel betrayed."

Shay and Robert Roop suggest you tap into your spouse's empathy: "If the first relationship sexually wasn't good, here's how not to destroy the second one."

You could even start with the top three turn-ons and the top three turnoffs in intimacy. This is especially important if your previous spouse asked or forced you to do things that were uncomfortable for you. Let your current spouse know. Be upfront and honest.

If you're uncomfortable or shy discussing sex with your spouse, then write it in a letter and pass that to your mate. Write an agenda: "This is what I would like to see in our lovemaking."

Another option is to purchase a good Christian sex book and mark the sections you want your spouse to read. Then pass the book, earmarked, and ask your spouse to read the earmarked pages. If your spouse is more comfortable responding in a letter, do it that way!

Do this with sensitivity, though. And women, be aware that men are more sensitive in this area.

The more you talk, the more comfortable you'll become.

5. Make foreplay an all-day event. Hug in the morning. Call each other during the day. Lock eyes and hold that gaze for several seconds. Take a shower and be clean! Shave your legs (or guys, shave your five o'clock shadow if your wife doesn't like facial hair). Take an interest in each other's day. Touch each other—a squeeze on the shoulder when you're walking past, a quick kiss on the neck. Hold hands just because.

6. Wives, get creative with your body. If body image is an issue for you, there are several things to try.

First, be aware that many men are not as offended by your stretch marks or "flawed" thighs. Women are more body conscious than men. When was the last time you noticed a man looking at his derriere in the mirror, wondering aloud if his pants make his hips look big?

Or is this your husband? When he's finished eating supper, he undoes his belt and pants button, leans back, groans, then gets up and walks around the house the rest of the evening that way? Do you honestly think he is concerned about his body image that night when he reaches for you to connect sexually? Uh, no.

If it helps, Shay Roop recommends you purchase a really pretty negligee that will cover your perceived "flaws." It's still sexy for your husband, and it makes you feel feminine. So if you're big busted with stretch marks from breastfeeding your seven children, get lingerie that's sheer at the bottom but has more covering at the top.

Have sex by candlelight or in the dark and take your time removing your clothing. By that point, your husband will probably be so aroused, he won't care if you think you're the size of an elephant.

7. Schedule sex. The unfortunate reality in remarriage where kids are around and the career is more established is that spontaneity goes out the window. If you want to have a sexual relationship with your spouse, you are going to have to schedule sex. Pick a night, put it on the calendar, and stick to it. That way you know it's a sex night and you can prepare for it.

8. Don't give up! If your sex life is still dragging along, needing CPR, don't bury it yet. Start praying about it. That's what Janie did. When her sex life was struggling, Janie decided, *If God asks me to pray about everything else, I'm going to start praying about my sex life too.* So every day she started to pray for her husband. "I prayed that God would bless him and our sex life. That God would work a miracle there."

Then she sat back and waited. "I started to see little sparks," she says. "That was exciting! They were small, but they were there." She readjusted her expectations and committed to praying daily for her sex life. "It's still not earth-shattering sex, but it's much better than it was. And we're enjoying each other so much more now that I've let God worry about it."

for *even* after

How do you know when to seek counseling?

Talking to a professional, Christian, third party is essential if an ex had an affair. The entire trust level has been lost. If your spouse does not want to have a sexual relationship, has an aversion to sex, or struggles with sex, seek counseling to work through that. "You can read all the self-help books you want," says Shay Roop. "But they are not going to help. Dealing with sexual issues goes deep and can bring intense pain, and that's simply not something that a person will be willing to do on his or her own without help."

Shay suggests that you backtrack a bit. Say, "I understand it's not personal. There's a stumbling block in our relationship. I understand that you need to work on this, and I'm willing to put sex on the back burner for a while."

13

money matters

{how to keep them from taxing you}

I've got all the money I'll ever need,
if I die by four o'clock.

Henny Youngman

When Dean and Beth were married, Dean had substantial debt and a huge monthly alimony/child support arrangement. Although Beth had been married before, she had no children and was debt free.

She and I spoke briefly before she and Dean married because she was feeling uneasy about acquiring his debt.

After hearing the entire story, I suggested that they postpone the wedding until he could at least pay down his outstanding IRS and credit card debt. However, they decided to continue with their wedding plans.

Now several years into their marriage, they have a horrible grasp on their finances. Beth now has a deep resentment against Dean's ex, who "continues to call and demand even more money."

In fact, in the divorce settlement, Dean gave his ex-wife the house. She allowed it to go into foreclosure because she didn't pay the mortgage with the money he sent every month specifically for that purpose.

"Dean's credit is shot. And she doesn't care! It's her fault," Beth says. "And what's worse, she's now taking my credit down too."

Studies show that finances are one of the top conflicts in marriage.

In a recent survey, pollsters found that divorce often comes with a financial penalty: 47 percent of respondents said divorce made their financial situation worse; 35 percent had to go into debt; 22 percent had to seek financial support from friends and family; 28 percent had to sell household items or personal assets; 27 percent had to sell or redeem financial investments; 44 percent said it was extremely difficult to save for post-secondary education for the children after divorce.[1]

Many of us enter remarriage in the red.

Five years into the marriage, Dean and Beth still don't feel like a team because Beth can't change her surname to Dean's (because of the debt issues). They have separate bank accounts, separate assets and property.

"How *could* we feel like a team under all this mess?" Beth says. "And the tension becomes greater when his ex-wife calls to complain or demand Dean pay for something else."

They're counting the days until the alimony and child support payments cease—but that's still two more years from now.

"The money issue has really taken a toll on our relationship," says Beth. "We entered our marriage with money challenges, and it's only gotten worse."

it's not about the money

Money is really not the problem. It's what we *do* with money that can cause problems. But the more important issue seems to be our attitudes about money. Those attitudes can determine the strength of our relationship.

When couples marry the first time, they are pretty much on equal footing financially—in that they don't owe child support, alimony, or have huge debt because of attorney fees and divorce settlement issues. But in remarriages, the divorced person is either dirt poor (studies show that divorced women typically get hit hardest financially) or is pretty well set—assets, established career, homeownership, car, furniture, goldfish, half of the ex's portfolio and retirement money.

So we enter remarriage a bit tentatively in regards to our finances. Because of our past experiences, we may deal with finances with defensiveness and suspicion. Or we may become more obsessive about the money, making sure there's a "yours," "mine," and "ours"—which may also fall under "mine."

This may cause some tension toward our spouse, especially if that spouse is more financially stable. We may choose to go the separate but equal route. There are benefits and challenges to each. So the question is, do we combine or not combine?

accounts: when one is better than two

When Sheila, a first-time bride, and her husband, James, were married, they decided that they would merge everything. "Love conquers any silly ol' money dispute" was their motto.

The benefit to that choice was that they were committed to working as a team. They were starting off their marriage on the right foot.

The challenge was that James had given his kingdom to his ex-wife in alimony and child support payments—which was now being covered by Sheila's money too.

"I couldn't believe how much we were paying," admits Sheila. "And that was my money too."

This is a question to hash out: is the stepparent going to pay some or all of the blended family's expenses, including alimony or child support expenses?

You need to concentrate on "ours," not "yours" and "mine"—especially when dealing with blended family issues: school functions, college, insurance. But also realize that if you combine, the ex can go to the court and siphon money from your paycheck and accounts.

to separate completely

Of course, the other option is to keep separate funds.

Angel and her husband, Steve, separate everything into the "yours" and "mine" category. Steve pays child support out of his account. They both write separate checks for utilities and everything else. If you think that sounds complicated, you're right. This is one area where it becomes very easy to build self-protective walls.

If assets remain in one spouse's name alone, there's no shared control. That could potentially lead to problems down the road with one spouse making all the decisions. It could lead one spouse to feel as if the other is withholding a part of him or herself. It could lead spouses to question trustworthiness. All of a sudden, you and your spouse are not "open books."

Leslie did this with her husband, Mark. She kept all her money separate from his. So when she needed a new car, she went out and bought one without discussing it with her husband.

"That doesn't draw me closer to Leslie," Mark told me. "I don't feel as though we're really doing life together."

If you have chosen to go this route, it may be a good idea to reopen the discussion with your spouse to make sure you're both still okay with this option.

to separate some

When Scott and I married, I moved to his home and town, which also meant I moved to his bank, where he was already established. Part of the problem was that his accounts used to be the same ones he shared with his ex-wife. I wasn't all that excited about sharing my money in accounts that his ex-wife could feasibly still gain access to because her name used to be on them, and she still knew the account numbers and his passwords.

So I compromised and placed my money in those accounts with my name added to them. But I kept a separate account for "fun money." This variation allows for the "ours" account, with separate, smaller luxury accounts for each of you.

A benefit is that you connect with each other as a team. The other benefit is that each of you has your own cash stash/fun money to do with as you please.

next steps

Whichever direction you choose to take, there are a few things to keep in mind that will keep your communication and marriage strong.

1. Mutually decide on a plan of action. Maybe your spouse decided to go with separate everything, but you are no longer comfortable with that. Talk about it. Give your reasons why. You may want to consider finding a good financial planner, especially one who has experience dealing with remarriage issues and understands all the different ramifications.

2. Wisely integrate assets. Think through what you want to integrate and what you want to keep separate.

3. Make financial decisions together. Even if you go the separate route, decide together on any major decisions—homes, cars, furniture, hot tubs, inground pools. Some couples put the limit at nothing over $25 unless they both are aware of and agree upon the purchase. This amount may be tough—especially since even small purchases like a sweater can cost more than $25. ("Hi, honey! I'm at Old Navy trying on bras. This one I want to buy is $27.95. Is that okay? It comes with a pair of underwear.")

Other couples go with $100. Or $200. Wherever you set that spending limit, make sure you're both okay with it.

4. Go over the accounts each month. Many times one person will feel more strongly about paying bills and balancing the checkbook. However, the other person needs to be kept updated on this each month. It's just a simple matter of respect and trust.

5. Discuss how you'll keep updated on each other's spending. If you both have ATM cards for the same account, place the receipts in a small bin or envelope and write those down as often as possible under one ledger.

6. No secrets. Make a commitment that no matter what, you won't keep secrets from each other.

realize money can trigger other issues

About three years ago, Carly found out that when she and her husband vacationed in Las Vegas, he lost four thousand dollars. He had to take out a loan to pay for it. And he never told her.

"My first husband lied about almost everything," says Carly. "So I was surprised when I caught Rick lying. He didn't outright lie, he just didn't tell me certain things."

But her discovery of what he'd done without telling her still took their relationship back a few steps.

"Before, I'd never had reason not to trust him," says Carly. "But when this came up, there was this little doubt that planted itself in my mind."

So she helped him pay off the loan, and everything seemed to be okay. Until last month.

Because Rick works third shift and is home during the day, he picks up and sorts the mail. But one day, Carly was home when the mail arrived, so she picked it up and noticed their bank statement had arrived. Wondering how much money they had in their account, she opened the envelope—to discover it was two loan statements that added up to twelve thousand dollars.

They had taken out a loan to pay for their wedding, but it was supposed to have been paid off in six months.

"We'd just talked about that loan," says Carly. "I'd said, 'This is going to be great to get this paid off. We'll have a little extra money each month.' And he never said anything!"

"What is this?" she asked Rick.

"Oh, it's nothing," he responded.

"Yeah," she said, "this is twelve thousand dollars."

"Well, those are the loans we had."

"No," she told him. "We had one loan—not two—and it's supposed to be paid off within the next few months."

Unbeknownst to Carly, Rick had some personal debt from before he remarried. Again, he never told her about it.

"He's very personal about his finances," she says. "He never likes anyone to know. He didn't want me to worry about it." So he borrowed money from his 401(k) and was working to pay it back.

But the big problem was that it popped up as an issue because her first husband was deceitful, and now she saw ways in which her second husband was being deceitful as well.

When Carly confronted Rick on it, he said, "I wasn't lying to you. I was going to tell you about it. You would never have known if you hadn't seen that."

Carly said, "Well, you did kind of lie because I said something the other day about the extra money we're going to have at the end of that month. But that's not true, we're not going to have that money. We're still going to be digging out from your loan. And you didn't say anything."

Then she dropped the bomb.

"If you ever wonder why I'm suspicious of you or I don't trust you, here you go."

Then she set a limit. "I told him, 'That's it. Anything like this ever happens again, anything financial at all, you're off everything. You will not have an ATM card to our account, your name will not be on the house. I will strip you of everything.'"

She was clear that it wasn't going to lead to a divorce. She told him, "It's never, 'I'm going to leave you.'" But she drew clear boundaries.

He agreed.

the costs of guilt

"I'm so frustrated with my husband," Penny told me one day over lunch. "He lets his kids get away with anything. They're so spoiled because he buys them whatever they want. He constantly gives them money. He has no boundaries with them."

"Why do you think that is?" I asked.

"Honestly," she told me, "I think it's because he still feels guilty over the divorce and breakup of his family, so he's trying to make up for it by buying them."

Penny nailed it.

I've seen more people frustrated because their mate lavishes funds on the children out of guilt over the past. What these spouses don't seem to realize is that money doesn't make the kids feel better. It simply eases the parent's guilty conscience. So the children may learn to manipulate and use the situation to get what they want. And it leaves the new spouse out in the cold.

"I have no problem with Jimmy spending money on the children for things they actually need," says Penny, "school items or whatever. But he gets them new techno-gadgets—the biggest and best—regardless of cost. In the meantime, I'm looking at our house that desperately needs updating and simple maintenance that we can't afford because both boys have to have great cell phones and the works."

I wish I had an easy answer for this one. Unfortunately, if you're the spouse with the guilt complex, you're probably also suffering from denial of the guilt complex. You shake your head and say, "That's ridiculous." If you're the other spouse, you feel frustrated because your mate won't listen to you and you feel dishonored and probably want to strangle her with a five dollar bill . . . except you can't because she's just spent it on Junior.

Instead of doing nothing or letting frustrations fester to a boiling point, try these constructive steps for a way of coping:

- **Discuss the problem in a calm and nonaccusatory way.**
  "I'm noticing that Harry's portion of the cell phone bill was

one hundred dollars. When we bought the phone we told him he had a set number of minutes and anything over that he would have to pay for himself. Yet, we continue to pay for those extra minutes. Is there anything we can do to rectify this?" That may work better than, "You lousy pig. Your kid is so irresponsible with his cell phone—and you don't do anything about it. You're protecting him! How's he ever gonna learn? You better do something about it."

- **Keep a log of your finances.** That way after a certain period of time, you can show your spouse the log and say, "I've been keeping track of our finances, and I want to show you something you may not be aware of. We average one hundred dollars each month on Harry's cell phone bill. That's on top of the three hundred in new clothes. The one hundred for his car insurance. The three hundred on the digital camera. The twenty bucks a week for gas. . . . That leaves us with ten dollars to pay our mortgage and eat. Are ramen noodles and water okay for you tonight?"
- **Pray about it.** Ask God to open your spouse's eyes to the root of the problem. But also ask God to give you patience and understanding and wise words to say at the right time.
- **Ask that a separate account be set up for the children.** Each week your spouse can put a certain amount of money in that account and dip into it whenever the guilty urge comes upon him. That way, it's not affecting your joint account.
- **Don't nag.** Pray about it, bring it up, then let it go. If your spouse continues down that path, wait for the right time to bring it up again constructively. Hint: that would not be in smart-aleck statements every fifteen minutes.

the will

Redo your will. Or create one—now's the time! If something should happen to your spouse and his old will left the house to his ex-wife, and he never rewrote the will . . . so sorry for you. Maybe she will allow you to rent a room . . . that small closet off the cellar.

Actually, putting a will together isn't too difficult. You can even download a do-it-yourself will from the internet. Being that I'm an old-fashioned kind of gal, I prefer going to an attorney (even though it is a bit more expensive). Do some research first online. Google "wills" or "trusts" or "estates," and you'll get a number of different sites that will answer any questions you may have about what you should do.

The important thing is to be as specific as possible. Exactly what you are giving to whom. An attorney can walk you through all of that.

We have a friend who is involved in an ugly estate battle with his stepbrothers and sister over his father's will. Do yourself, your kids, your family pet, and everyone else a favor and spell out your desires.

the emergency fund

I don't know about you, but I feel more secure with a "rainy day" savings account. If you're living paycheck to paycheck, that can cause a lot of stress on a marriage. But having money socked away can save heartache and anxiety when emergencies arise. Start by putting money into a "no touch" savings account. Then build up to one thousand dollars and work up to three to six months of salary. This should be liquid assets. Cash. And it's for emergencies only—for instance, your car's transmission went out while you were driving in the Arizona desert. An emergency is not paying the credit cards, taking your office staff out to dinner, buying your daughter an Easter outfit, or buying anything on eBay—no matter how cool it is.

Regardless of where you are financially, make a commitment to always tell the truth about money. Talk about it. Talk about your expectations, plan for the future, and discuss ways to get there without going into debt.

for *even* after

Create a luxury account. I call this my "this is my money, keep your paws off" account. Or, more nicely put, it's my "fun money" account.

This is money I spend on my lunches, gas, and any extras, such as clothing or chick flick movies with my girlfriends. It's mine, and I don't have to answer to, consult with, explain to, or justify to anyone about how I spend it.

But also, once it's gone, it's gone.

My husband has one too. We both love it because we don't have to give each other an "allowance." And it's one less financial issue that could be a conflict in many marriages.

14

what's up with that?

{dealing with all the other issues}

If only we stopped trying to be happy,
we could have a pretty good time.

Edith Wharton, novelist

There are a few advantages to a remarriage. You've been through marriage one time already, so you know what the issues are. Even though some are going to be bigger than others in different marriages, the issues are basically the same in remarriages: communication, finances, sex, children, ex-spouses. There are also the smaller issues that many times we don't take as seriously or discuss as thoroughly.

dump the former house!

One of the biggest mistakes Sally made in her marriage was moving into her husband's house—the home he shared with his previous wife.

we will build a new house

"The emotional land mines were everywhere," says Sally. "We slept in *her* bed. I used *her* pots and pans. The decorating was in *her* taste. Every time I turned around, I was reminded that I was Wife Number Two."

Before Scott and I were married, we discussed where we would live and finally decided, against my instincts, that I would move into his house, because we were eventually planning to tear it down to rebuild.

I tried to think about the big picture—in a few years I would have a new house. But as much as I tried, those years before the rebuild were tolerable at best and hellish at worst. I never felt as though the house was mine. It was Scott's house. I just happened to live there with him. It was as though I were a tenant, not a home owner.

While some people can make the old house work for them—through remodeling or redecorating—most of the time it becomes an albatross in the remarriage. As the newbie, you are constantly aware that your spouse and the children have memories that predate the new marriage. And while you may have decided to make the sacrifice because the children will feel more comfortable and more stable if they're not uprooted, that decision may work against you. The newcomer may be viewed as an intruder, as the ghost of the previous mate still haunts the house.

When Sally wanted to update and decorate the house to suit her tastes and style, she met with resistance, and it became clear that it was her husband's house. "I felt left out and uncomfortable in my own home," she says.

A lot of Eileen's frustration came when she discovered her husband's ex still felt she could enter the house whenever she desired—even after her husband told the ex the house was off limits.

"Lee's ex would walk in the house and head for her daughter's bedroom, as if it were still her home!" says Eileen. "I'd stand at the front door, frozen. I felt threatened and shocked that she thought she could do that."

So Lee had another conversation with his ex and with his daughter. "Imagine my surprise," says Eileen, "when I discovered his ex was *still* doing it even after the second conversation, only this time when we weren't around to catch her. She'd leave little clues she was there or would say subtle things about my decorating that she couldn't know unless she had been in the house."

When Eileen brought up the situation to her husband, he brushed it off, saying, "I talked to both my ex and my daughter, and they know that's not acceptable."

"He wouldn't believe me!" says Eileen. "So basically, it was my word against his daughter and ex-wife's, and I came out on the bottom." That is, until one day when Lee arrived home from work early and found his ex in his house.

"That was the best day of my life," says Eileen. "He told his ex if she ever stepped foot in the house again, he would call the police. Too bad she never tried it again."

You may encounter some obstinacy along the way as well. One woman tried to rearrange the family kitchen. Since she was shorter than the first wife, she placed things, such as the salt shaker, on lower shelves where she could reach them. But when she would reach for the salt shaker, she would find it back on a higher shelf. She wasn't sure if her stepchildren were just doing that out of habit or if they were being difficult.[1] Or the stepchildren may not like when you rearrange the furniture, or how you set "their" table, or where you move photographs. You may hear, "This is where we've always had it" or "We never put it that way before."

If you're currently living in the "ex" house, here's my suggestion: move. Move for the sake of your sanity, your self-esteem, and your marriage. Move into a house with joint ownership where you both will feel free to create your own style as a couple.

You will not have to compete with the ex or with any memories—you will get to make new ones! You will avoid countless conflicts, frustration, and hurt if you move. This is about giving your new life together a fighting chance.

171

If you choose not to move, you will need to navigate some difficult waters between the memories of the children and possibly your spouse. If you do nothing else, change the décor of the master bedroom. Get rid of the bed, the bedspread, or anything else that the ex had his or her hands on. The ghost of the ex can linger in the kitchen and family room if you want, but *kick him or her out of your bedroom.*

A word of caution: change your bedroom completely and as soon as possible. However, you may want to make changes throughout the rest of the house gradually, so that they are almost imperceptible.

I kept much of the décor in Scott's house status quo in order for his daughter to feel more comfortable. But gradually I would add a photograph here and there or take down an ugly wall hanging his ex-wife had. To my relief, Scott was agreeable and helpful in trying to make me feel comfortable in his house. To his credit, he did a good job, as best he could. But a lot of my feelings stemmed from me, not from him. And I just wanted out of that house!

In her book *Ex-Wives and Ex-Lives*, author Paula J. Egner has this to say about living with the ghost of the ex: "Exorcise those old memories by refusing to let them languish at the death scene of his former marriage. You wouldn't expect your new blended family to live there had an actual murder occurred, would you?"[2] I think that's well put, don't you?

where to worship

Along with the house dilemma, there is the church dilemma. If you are attending the former church and feel comfortable worshiping there, great! Kudos to you. However, this may be another situation in which you and your spouse find a new church home where you can worship together without the ghost of the ex sitting in the pew next to you.

This is actually an issue that Scott and I are currently grappling with. While we love our church home and are involved in ministry there, we seem to constantly "run into" his ex-wife (which seems quite a feat considering our church has more than twenty thousand members and we don't run into anyone else we know as much as we do her). After a recent episode that was incredibly uncomfortable and confrontational for Scott and me, we reintroduced the topic of finding a new church home.

Honestly, the prospect of leaving the place we love makes us grieve. Yet, for us, we feel that we worship better when we are not constantly looking over our shoulder for fear that you-know-who is watching.

This is a situation that I encourage you both to spend a lot of time praying about. Ask God to give you peace and clarity as you decide what to do.

memory triggers

Inevitably something at some point will appear that will trigger a mental tape from the previous marriage. It may be something involving finances: his ex-wife was a shopaholic and charged up a thirty-thousand-dollar credit card bill, so now when you ask to use the credit card to buy gasoline, he flips. Or her ex-husband was a cheater, and when you show up ten minutes late after work, she reads you the riot act. Those are times when we need to stop, take a few deep breaths, and ask, "What's really going on here?"

Many times the past can cause us to become hypervigilant about anything and everything—even superficial, insignificant things can be blown out of proportion and wreak havoc.

These are the times to communicate honestly about what's going on in your head. Communicate your fears, even if they seem irrational as you're speaking them. We can stuff away that pain or we can confront it. If we work through it, eventually we will conquer it and it will not bother us anymore. It's always important for us to make our new spouse aware of what's happening.

Once we recognize those memory triggers, we can be proactive. When I'm out of town or running late, for instance, I try to call Scott just to touch base. I let him know where I am and what I'm doing. I try to respect that sometimes his old mental tapes are going to replay. I never want to give him a reason not to trust me, so I try to head off the triggers before they happen.

Ask your spouse to share with you some ways you can recognize the memory triggers and what you can do to lessen the impact on your relationship. Reaching out in that way will strengthen the bonds and trustworthiness in your marriage.

who are you?

The first time Scott accidentally called me by his ex-wife's name was in front of his daughter. Oh yes, I could have throttled him. I was mortified. And what was worse, he didn't realize he'd done it.

The second time was in front of his family at dinner. It slipped out of his mouth, and he realized it right away. Of course, so did everyone else at the dining room table.

In the more than ten years Scott and I have been together, he's slipped up only those two times. But that hasn't made me hurt any less. Both of those times I have been faced with a choice: I can take it personally and think he still pines for his ex, or I can take it at face value and understand that habits die hard and that's all it is, a habit.

Fortunately, I chose to look at it as a habit. It's the same thing as when your mother can't get your name straight and calls you by your sister's name. My mom would keep calling me "Page," our Dalmatian's name. Does that mean my mother was thinking about Page? Does it mean she was wishing I was the dog? I hardly think so, although I should probably ask her about that . . .

Here's the deal: there's a strong chance that at some point in your relationship, he is going to slip up and call you by the ex's name. That does not mean he's thinking of her, or wishing they were together again. Nor does it mean he is comparing the two of you. He slipped up—that's all. When those times happen, give each other grace. And double up your efforts on calling each other by your first names, rather than pet names. Using your actual name will hardwire it into your spouse's brain for future reference. (There's only one time when red flags should go up with name calling, and that's during sex. If your spouse blurts out the ex's name in the middle of your lovemaking, take that seriously. There are some unresolved issues that your spouse will need to deal with professionally.)

comparisons

Did you ever play that game that goes, "One of these things is not like the other . . ."? I always loved that game. You have to look closely at the scenes or objects and scrutinize and compare them until you find the one that is unique in some way.

In a remarriage, most of the comparisons should have happened before you and your spouse said "I do." But let's be honest, there will be certain times when a comparison is unavoidable. During those times, unless your current spouse comes out favorably in the comparison, keep your thoughts to yourself.

If you feel your spouse is comparing *you* to the ex, tell her, without accusing her, how hurt you feel when she mentions her ex. If she continues, turn her criticisms into positives: "Yes, I am different from Bob. He loved to go out and socialize or go to the movies, and I prefer to stay home and spend more time with you." Or you could say simply, "I don't do comparisons."

In Carly's first marriage, her husband worked minutes from their home, while Carly worked twenty miles away. "When I'd get home," she says, "he'd be sitting in the living room, waiting for me to make a decision about that evening's meal. He never offered to cook, go to the grocery store, start supper." Contrast that with her current husband, who is a cook. "He won't let me in the kitchen to get a glass of water when he's cooking!" Carly says. "He'll get it for me and bring it to me. I'd still love him if he didn't cook, but, gosh, it sure is nice! And I've made a point of telling him that often."

If you've been married before, it's good for your current spouse to be reinforced verbally, because I'm sure he wonders about the first spouse. Even though you may talk negatively enough about your ex for him to understand that there's no comparison between the two mates, it's still good to bring up what the current spouse does well that the former spouse didn't when you feel it is appropriate. "When I tell my husband about his cooking," says Carly, "that this is something I never had before, it brings him confidence in the marriage. He's providing something unique to our marriage."

Jennifer agrees: "You can't help but compare the current with the former, but it doesn't have to be something bad. Since I remarried, I have compared my marriage and my second husband to my first experience with continuous gratitude and appreciation. Even after five years, I am still amazed at how wonderful certain aspects of this marriage are. I love that my husband is home every night, that he takes an interest in projects around the home, that he does dishes every day and cleans up after himself—I can't help but appreciate how things are different! Comparisons have been a wonderful way for me to appreciate my husband verbally almost every day for how new and blessed my life has become by being married to him!"

for *even* after

In today's culture, drifting apart is a simple process
that does not demand a whole lot of effort. . . .
Growing apart is almost a silent cause of death in a

second marriage. The only prevention is spending quality time together and scheduling time for it every week on your calendar.[3]

—Jim Smoke

You have to be intentional in marriage. Scott and I can feel when our marriage starts to drift. So we claim Saturday mornings as our reconnect time. But also, just recently, we decided that for an hour after supper every night, we would play Scrabble together. These have been great connection times for us.

15

happily *even* after

{yes, a fairy tale can come true}

See, I am doing a new thing! Now it springs up;
do you not perceive it? I am making a way in the desert
and streams in the wasteland.

Isaiah 43:19

Recently my friend Carmen told me about a beautiful experience she had when she was dating her soon-to-be-second husband. One day as they were walking down the street they passed a florist shop. Her husband-to-be, Dave, stopped at the window and said, "Those are beautiful red roses."

"No, they're not," Carmen told him.

"Yes, they're beautiful red roses."

"No," she said. "Red roses are what men give to women when they've been cheating on them. I hate red roses."

They continued walking, and she didn't think any more about it. But later in their relationship, when Dave decided Carmen was "the one," he sent her flowers—a huge bouquet of yellow roses. The note attached said, "I will never give you a reason to get red roses from me."

In remarriage, we have the unique ability to bring trust and healing to a broken person in a way no one else can.

We understand that marriage isn't easy. And remarriage is no piece of cake either. But remarriage offers us a wonderful opportunity to live out grace, forgiveness, and joy—especially if we make the choice to live that way. Former first lady Martha Washington once said, "I have learned from experience that the greater part of our happiness or misery depends on our dispositions and not on our circumstances." *yes!*

compatibility is not an issue

On our last anniversary, Scott not-so-subtly placed a cut-out newspaper article on the kitchen counter. At the top of the article was a photo of Ralph and Alice Kramden from the classic TV sitcom *The Honeymooners*. Directly under that in large, bold letters the title blurted out, "Marital Bliss? It Isn't Natural."

The first paragraph stated, "A growing body of research suggests there is no such thing as a compatible couple."

"Is there something you want to tell me?" I asked as I glanced over at him.

"Just read the article."

The article went on to quote Ted Huston, a professor of psychology and human ecology, who has been studying 168 married couples since the 1980s. He said, "Compatibility is misunderstood and overrated."[1]

To which both Scott and I say a hearty "Amen!"

The truth is that in many ways Scott and I are incompatible. Sure, we share a lot of common interests and hold the same values. But we are so different in so many ways!

Feel that way about your mate?

If you do, know that you are normal—and that God designed it that way. There's a divine reason why "men are from Mars and women are from Venus." When we meld together in marriage, we can become complete, learning from, challenging, encouraging, and serving each other. That's God's will for us. But it takes work, and God allows us to choose whether or not that plan will be successful.

I'll never forget one letter I received at *Marriage Partnership*: "My marriage ended because we had become 'incompatible.' Rather than working on our problems, we decided to continue to grow apart and end with a divorce." She understood that marriage is about choice, and the decision is ours to make. Even Billy Graham understands the truth about marriage when he states: "Ruth and I are happily incompatible."[2]

Even for the most incompatible couple there's hope. Ron Deal, founder of Smart Stepfamilies, reminds us that "there is a honeymoon for remarried couples, but it comes at the end of the journey, after seven to nine years."[3]

That means we need to hang in there, through the difficult "adjustment" period. Through these years I've learned that my marriage is at its worst when I allow it to be. My attitude makes all the difference. When I decide to control my mind-set, it doesn't matter what Scott does or doesn't do; I'm okay and thus our marriage is okay.

I read somewhere once that remarriage, more than first marriages, is about making the new spouse feel secure. This made me realize we have a lot more power over our relationship than we give ourselves credit for.

It's important in our marriages not to blame our spouse for everything that we think they need to change or work on. We need to own up to our "stuff," to look at our own thoughts, actions, and reactions.

We can ask, beg, cajole, plead, manipulate, threaten, and use sex to force our spouse to change. (Which I don't recommend doing!) But the reality is that we can't change our spouse to be more like what we want. Sometimes acceptance becomes the reality.

The one comfort is that even God won't force someone to change. But he can soften a heart. He can help us accept what we can't change and find joy and gratitude in the midst of our circumstances.

Carly understands this concept. She says, "When we hit a rough road recently, I discovered I didn't have to think, *Oh, is this the end of the marriage?* Instead I thought, *Okay, we're going to work through this.* That makes a big difference in our relationship."

Is that really doable? Yes! Gary Smalley tells us, "God gave you the power to choose. So when it comes to how you will respond in a relationship that has hit some rough waters, never tell yourself, 'I have no choice!' That's a lie. The truth is, you *do* have a choice. Lots of choices."[4]

Like many aspects of remarriage, a great deal of maturity is required to do this well, perhaps more than most of us can muster on a good day. Yet we are not alone; God walks this path with us, offering us hope and help. Pastor and author Charles Swindoll reminds us,

> The One who understands your deepest longing and most private burdens cares about your pain and can identify with your disappointment. His name is Jesus. He knows all the reasons you feel you'd be better off walking away from your marriage. Still, he stands alongside you today, not ready to wag his divine finger and scold you for your lack of faith, but eager to calm and comfort you, help you think even deeper, and bring a fresh resolve to trust him for another day.[5]

keep your faith first

Want to grow closer to each other? Pray together. Get involved in a small group or a church that provides ministry for remarried couples.

The biggest difference between Jennifer's first and second marriages is her shared faith with her second husband, in that they have purposefully made prayer a regular part of their marriage.

"We pray together either first thing in the morning or right before we go to sleep," says Jennifer. "I can call him at work with a crisis in a friend's life or when I am upset about something, and we will pray right then together on the phone. Prayer is such a deep intimacy in our marriage."

If you can't pray together, pray individually. Pray for your spouse, that God would bless him in his work, in his health, in his relationships, and in your marriage. Pray for blessings upon him.

A friend of mine, Chris Armstrong, writes this about the importance of having a solid faith throughout your marriage:

> We can't load all of our needs for emotional sustenance and spiritual meaning into a single relationship. God didn't make us that way. Whether we focus all our needs for affection and support on a spouse or even on God himself, we are bound to be disappointed—and the temptation may be irresistible to turn elsewhere, to unsanctioned human relationships, to fill the void. This is not because God cannot meet our emotional needs. Rather, he designed us to have them met in a range of human relationships. In short, his "law of love" is cross-shaped. Without either the vertical or the horizontal beam, its structure fails.[6]

couples who laugh together last

One of the most surprising things I discovered after Scott and I were married was how funny he is. He cracks me up constantly! He has this dry, straight-line delivery that catches me off guard every time.

I'm sad to say I didn't see much of his humor when we were dating. I asked him about that several years after we were married, and he said, "It's amazing how divorce can suck the laughter out of you." Yet Proverbs 17:22 says, "A cheerful heart is good medicine, but a crushed spirit dries up the bones."

"So why the change?" I asked.

He smiled and said, "Because I feel safe again."

The other day we were complaining about how we feel that we have to call our siblings if we want to get together with them. I said, "We get more calls from your ex-wife than we do from all your siblings put together." We both started laughing, and it made light of our remarried situation.

I love to hear my husband laugh. It brings such joy to me. It makes me want to do everything I can to keep him jovial, because it brings a lightness to our marriage.

I love to hear you laugh

lobby for hobbies

One great way to connect with each other is to try new hobbies. The other day, I told Scott I wanted us to learn how to ballroom dance. After he finished laughing at the prospect, he nodded quietly.

That's a good sign, I thought. *He didn't say no right away.*

We've had fun learning how to build a house, hike a mountain trail, study real estate, and learn photography. We love to read books aloud to each other. Within the next few years, we plan to breed our dog, build another house, hike the trails in Yellowstone and Glacier national parks, motorcycle across the country, and ballroom dance (I haven't let Scott forget about that last one!). Some of the things we try we realize are not for us. But they still offer us a time to bond, so they are still worth the adventure.

Why not set out to volunteer together? Join a local community volleyball or softball league. Learn to golf or fish or hike or rock climb together. Take a gourmet cooking class, a pottery or a photography class at a local community college. Even if you don't enjoy the hobby, you can still enjoy the time together.

Just hang out together. I love just being with my husband. We don't have to do anything special; I just like having him near me. He offers me safety, comfort, and security.

Several weeks ago, my heart broke when I read a response to a *Marriage Partnership* poll question about how couples spend time together. One woman wrote simply, "Unfortunately, we do not make any time together anymore . . ." I read that short sentence, got up from my desk, closed my office door, and cried. I felt her sadness and remorse. There was no anger; it was almost a resigned statement.

Please don't allow your marriage to get to that point. Fight for your marriage. Start by fighting for it with prayer. Ask God to melt hearts and open minds, to help you and your spouse be willing to take baby steps toward each other.

act *as if* . . .

If you are struggling in your remarriage, act as if you aren't. In other words, treat your spouse as if you are happily married. While I realize this may be difficult to do, acting "as if" you have good feelings toward your spouse can have surprising results. The more you perform this action, the more it becomes part of your "feelings." The apostle Paul talked about it this way: "Bear with each other and forgive whatever grievances you may have against one another. Forgive as the Lord forgave you. And over all these virtues put on love, which binds them all together in perfect unity" (Colossians 3:13–14).

Write down your spouse's good qualities. Make a list of all the good things that initially attracted you to your spouse. Read the list daily—several times a day—and say it aloud if you have to!

Throughout Scripture, God tells us how important remembering is. It stands to reason, then, that the same tactics would work for our spouses. Remember the times you "felt" warmly toward your spouse. Remember the things your spouse did for you that brought warm feelings.

Recently, Scott and I met with a woman whose husband is serving time in a federal prison. Her life will forever be changed because of the illegal choices he made. While many people have encouraged her to divorce him, she has chosen to remember daily the good things about their marriage. "Sure, I'm angry with him. He has ruined us financially, we have to move when he's released, and he will be blacklisted for the rest of his life. But do I forget all the good aspects of him and remember this one thing?" she asked us. "Is that what God does to us?" Let's be honest, acting "as if" is more brave than bailing. And in the end, it's the more honorable thing to do.

Remember that marriage is a work in progress. Your relationship will never "arrive." There will always be growing and learning to do. Take the risk! Don't allow this marriage—or your children—to become another statistic.

it's the little things

There's something that happens when Scott's eyes meet mine and hold them for a few seconds. It's a magical connection, and I feel the entire world melt away. It's such a simple thing. It takes no energy, no words, just a little effort. But what results! When we lock eyes, especially when other people are around, I feel as though we're a team: it's us against the world.

For Jennifer, it's when she or her husband admits when they're wrong.

Touch each other. Cradle your mate's hand, stroke a cheek, kiss the top of her head, touch his shoulder, pat an arm. Be intentional and touch at least three times a day. Be your spouse's advocate, and always respect each other's privacy.

Scott and I cuddle in the mornings. We spoon while the alarm goes off fifty times, and we say, "Five more minutes." It isn't about the extra sleep. It's about making a silent connection first thing in the morning.

Katie and her husband write love notes to each other to connect. "Some days it's more like 'barely like' notes," she says. "But we've followed through on that commitment. But even those notes have been especially helpful on a day when I'm feeling down or when my husband has to travel for business. I pull out those letters and feel immediately connected to him."

Make your spouse the first person you greet when you come home from work. Kiss him and tell him how nice it is to see him. It's the little things that add up.

safeguardings

After Janet's unfaithfulness in her first marriage, she self-imposed boundaries without her second husband even asking her to. "I am accountable to my husband about where I am, whom I meet at out-of-town conferences, and who I send email to," says Janet. There are no secrets, and he has total access into every area of her life. "We have given each other permission to ask any question, any time. The only rule is that we must be honest, even if it is difficult. That means I can ask him what he's been viewing on the internet or what he watched on television at the hotel when he is out of town, and I know that he will be honest with me."

Set up boundaries on what you and your spouse will do. Ask each other difficult, honest questions. Promise that you'll work to make your marriage one of soul mates, not role mates.

The good news is that for Christians, the old has passed, the new has come. You may not have been first. Or your spouse may not have been your first.

The statistics for failed second and third marriages are pretty dismal. But they're just that: statistics. They are not you, nor your marriage. With God's help, and your determination, you *can* beat the statistics to live happily ever after, happily *even* after.

for *even* after

At church several months ago, our pastor talked
about love, using that famous section of Scripture,
1 Corinthians 13. He had us repeat an exercise that I
have since tried to recite every week. It's an amazing

187

"heart check." Read 1 Corinthians and replace the words *love is* with *I am*. After you read the passage, ask yourself, *Are these things becoming true of me?*

I am patient and kind.

I am not jealous or boastful or proud or rude.

I do not demand *my* own way.

I am not irritable, and *I* keep no record of when *I* have been wronged.

I am never glad about injustice but rejoice whenever the truth wins out.

I never give up, never lose faith.

I am always hopeful, and *I* endure through every circumstance (NLT).

notes

even after land

1. www.barna.org.
2. In-house *Marriage Partnership* demographic study.

chapter 1: against all odds

1. Stepfamily Association of America, www.allaboutfamilies.org.
2. Jim Watkins, "Top Ten Reasons I'm Not Divorcing My Wife," 1996, http://watkins
.gospelcom.net/divorce.htm.

chapter 2: CSI divorce

1. Dr. Les Carter, *Grace and Divorce* (San Francisco: Jossey-Bass, 2005), 151.
2. Sheila Wray Gregoire, *Honey, I Don't Have a Headache Tonight* (Grand Rapids:
Kregel, 2004), 40.
3. Gary Smalley, *The DNA of Relationships* (Wheaton: Tyndale, 2004), 38.
4. Ibid., 23.
5. Gary Oliver, "The Upside of Failure," *Marriage Partnership*, Summer 1996, 32.
6. Jim Smoke, "Special Tasks in a Second Marriage," *The Complete Marriage Book*, eds.
Dr. David Stoop and Dr. Jan Stoop (Grand Rapids: Revell, 2002), 258–59.
7. David Yount, "There's Really No Such Thing as No-Fault Divorce," Scripps Howard
News Service, November 13, 2004.

chapter 3: the GOD factor

1. Ted Olsen, compiler, "Go Figure," *Christianity Today*, November 2004, 22.
2. Smalley, *The DNA of Relationships*, 32.
3. Alister McGrath, ed., *The NIV Thematic Reference Bible* (Grand Rapids: Zondervan,
1999), 1030.
4. Everett Worthington Jr., *Forgiving and Reconciling*, rev. ed. (Downer's Grove, IL:
InterVarsity Press, 2003), 102. Many thanks to Everett Worthington Jr., from whom I've
borrowed several of my ideas on forgiveness, especially in remarriage.

chapter 4: forgiveness

1. Julie Ann Barnhill, *Radical Forgiveness* (Wheaton: Tyndale, 2004), 116.
2. Worthington, *Forgiving and Reconciling*, 132–33.
3. Barnhill, *Radical Forgiveness*, 112–13.
4. Worthington, *Forgiving and Reconciling*, 108.
5. Ibid., 133.

chapter 5: all the good-byes

1. Georgia Shaffer, "What I Wish I'd Known Before I Got Divorced," *Marriage Partnership*, Summer 2005, 47.
2. Ibid.
3. Quotes from Shay and Robert Roop are taken from personal interviews.

chapter 6: oh, lonesome, loser me

1. Carter, *Grace and Divorce*, 7.

chapter 7: the ex factor

1. Paula J. Egner, *Ex-Wives and Ex-Lives* (Jackson, TN: Aptly Spoken Enterprises, 2004), 22.
2. Ibid., 34.

chapter 8: the stepparent trap

1. Shaffer, "What I Wish I'd Known *Before* I Got Divorced," *Marriage Partnership*, 48.
2. Ylonda Gault Caviness, "His, Mine, Ours," *Essence*, December 2002, 152.
3. Ibid.

chapter 9: family dealings

1. Margaret Broersma, *Daily Reflections for Stepparents*, 2nd ed. (Grand Rapids: Kregel, 2003), 55.
2. Smoke, "Special Tasks in a Second Marriage," 266.

part 3: your marriage

1. Oliver, "The Upside of Failure," 33–34.

chapter 11: avoiding the communication crisis

1. Smoke, "Special Tasks in a Second Marriage," 259.
2. John Gottman, "Can't Get Rid of Your Problems?" *Marriage Partnership*, Spring 2002, 9.

chapter 12: sex

1. *Marriage Partnership* unpublished survey.

2. Dr. Harry R. Jackson, Jr., *In-Laws, Outlaws, and the Functional Family* (Ventura, CA: Gospel Light Publications, 2002), 196.

chapter 13: money matters

1. Conducted by Investors Group and Decima Research of divorced Canadians. Reported in Smartmarriages.com newsletter, July 19, 2004.

chapter 14: what's up with that?

1. Jeffrey Zaslow, "Moving in Can Be a Difficult Transition for a Second Spouse," *Wall Street Journal*, Oct. 20, 2004, reported in www.smartmarriages.com newsletter, October 21, 2004.

2. Egner, *Ex-Wives and Ex-Lives*, 85.

3. Smoke, "Special Tasks in a Second Marriage," 263–64.

chapter 15: happily *even* after

1. *Chicago Sun-Times*, November 5, 2004.

2. "You Said It," *Marriage Partnership*, Winter 2005, 7.

3. Ron Deal, in an interview with Michael J. McManus, printed in "A Perfect Christmas Gift—For a Stepparent," *Advance*, December 9, 2004, column #1,215.

4. Smalley, *The DNA of Relationships*, 33.

5. Charles R. Swindoll, *Getting Through the Tough Stuff* (Nashville: W Publishing Group, 2004), 78.

6. Chris Armstrong, "The Roots of Pentecostal Scandal: Romanticism Gone to Seed," www.christianitytoday.com/history/newsletter/2004/sep16.html.

Ginger Kolbaba is managing editor of *Marriage Partnership* magazine and previously was associate editor of *Today's Christian Woman*. She's also the author of *Dazzled to Frazzled and Back Again: The Bride's Survival Guide* and Gold Medallion nominated coauthor with Brian Birdwell and Mel Birdwell of *Refined by Fire: A Family's Triumph of Love and Faith*. Ginger and husband, Scott, live in Elgin, Illinois. To visit Ginger, to to www.GingerKolbaba.com.